Under the shade of Our Lady's sweet image

The story of a unique coastal parish in the Diocese of Down and Connor

Duane Fitzsimons

In honour of my ancestors:
those who tilled the land,
lifted the quill,
and wove this tapestry

Contents

Preface 9

One .... The first reformation............................ 11

Two .... The Reformation.................................. 21

Three .... The building of Chapeltown............................ 37

Four............... Building the second chapel 49

Five................ Continuing efforts within the parish 57

Six.................. Mount Saint Clement............................ 71

Seven............. The Little Sisters of Jesus 77

Eight.............. Notable parishioners............................ 81

         – William Sawey

         – Dr. William Hamilton Smyth

         – William Curran

         – Francis Joseph Bigger

         – Richard Francis Fitzsimons

Nine .... Vocations from the parish 99

Ten .... Priests since 1791 129

Eleven .... Sheepland 163

Twelve............ Saint Patrick's Well............................ 167

Thirteen .... Ardtole Church 173

Fourteen .... Our Lady of Dunsford 181

Bibliography 193

There was a Mission in Dunsford. It began on May the 9th 18
It lasted for two weeks. 1880

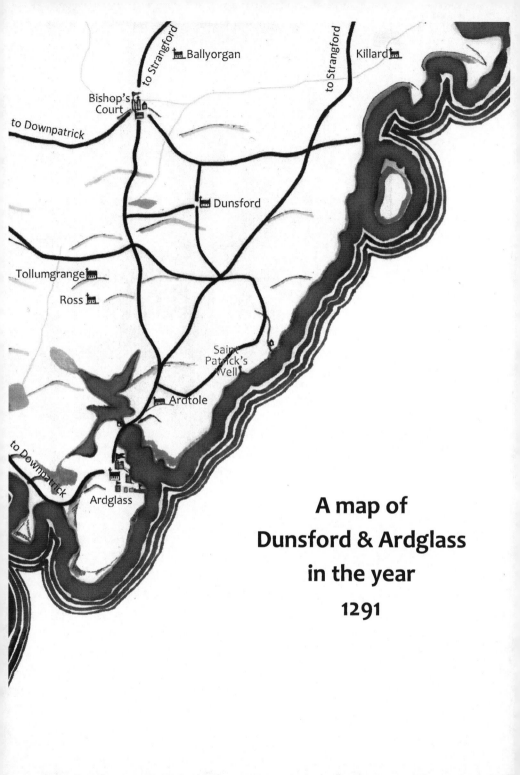

to Strangford
Ballyorgan
to Strangford
Killard
Bishop's
Court
to Downpatrick
Dunsford
Tollumgrange
Ross
Saint
Patrick's
Well
Ardtole
to Downpatrick
Ardglass

**A map of
Dunsford & Ardglass
in the year
1291**

Preface

My home parish of Dunsford and Ardglass is nestled on the east coast of County Down in a unique part of Ireland called the Lecale peninsula. It is where the island's national apostle, Saint Patrick, began and ended his mission. This work has stemmed from years of study into the heritage of Lecale, and a meeting with the Rev. Fr. Gerard McCloskey in December 2014. I was at that time keen to understand more about the history surrounding the survival of Our Lady of Dunsford. Believe it or not, it is the only pre-reformation stone statue of its kind on the entire island and therefore, also the oldest.

During this year we will mark the anniversary of the first Mass to be celebrated in Saint Mary's at Chapeltown two hundred and twenty five years ago. I believe it is timely that we should stop and look back on the journey that we have made to this point. We stand today on the cusp of a bright new future for the church. The great contribution of members from this parish through the years to the development of the church throughout this country, and on shores further afield, is a new angle which has remained undocumented thus far. This new volume will in itself make a very substantial contribution to this story.

A great deal of this work would not have been possible had it not been for that keen collector of local history snippets who was my grandfather, Henry Fitzsimons. He passed away in 2009 but it is thanks to his collection that I had a foundation on which to begin this work. I am pleased to bring to you an enhanced history of the other ecclesiastical sites in the parish which were incorporated into the fabric of the chapel built in 1791 by the Rev. Fr. Edward Mulholland. I, like him, will intertwine and marry original items into one work. In order to do this, documents and artefacts in both local and national custody have been perused.

The narrative of this text has been greatly assisted by the efforts of George Rice who, twenty five years ago, first recorded the history of Saint Mary's for its bicentenary. Since first meeting George in 2013 he has become a true friend and willing assistant in recording the history of this and other parts of Lecale. In addition to George's help I have also been greatly assisted by my father, Tony.

Likewise, I extend gratitude to those members of the parish who have assisted the project, namely Maire Bell, my cousins Maurice and Pat Fitzsimons, Mairead Gilchrist, Maureen Gill-Sharp, Seamus Gracey, Michael Howland, Bernadette Killen, Sean McAlea, and Willie Mulhall.

My gratitude must further extend to Clive Scoular and Thomas Johnston who have encouraged me in this work. They have assisted with the proof reading, layouts, and publication. I am very proud to be able to bring to you, the reader, sources from the Fitzsimons family archive such as the diary of Richard Clark, my great-great-great-grandfather, his son William's record of parish events, the biography of the Most Rev. Dr. William Crolly, Archbishop of Armagh, and the photographic collection of John MacMahon.

Duane Fitzsimons
Crossmore, Easter 2016

Right: Anglo Norman sarcophagus lid fragment preserved at Saint Mary's Church of Ireland, Dunsford.

ONE
The first reformation

Since the time Saint Patrick preached in this land, numerous churches and monastic settlements have been founded. Some in existence today can even claim to have been founded by the patron saint himself. Within the modern boundaries of this parish of Dunsford and Ardglass, there is one such site, Ardtole church, which can lay claim to having such an ancient foundation. Another site of antiquity is the Mullaghban, which, like so many other sites, bore the brunt of pillages by Norsemen in the latter half of the first millennium of the Christian church. The descendants of these Norsemen first came to Ireland on the invitation of Dermot MacMurrough in 1169. They arrived in vessels no different from those of their forebears but they went by the name of Normans.

The greatest sea change in the livelihoods of the inhabitants of Lecale came in January 1177 when John de Courcy arrived with his army in the middle of the night and seized Downpatrick. Then it was the capital of Uladh, an area roughly covering counties Down and Antrim. John de Courcy hailed from a noble Norman family who had their main English seat at Stogursey, otherwise known as 'the place of Courcy' in old English, located in Somerset. His father was in control of the administration of the family's lands in Yorkshire but, as his second son, John never stood to rise to much. Throughout John's formative years, England was constantly under revolution with power shifting from one prince to another. The situation was even more precarious in Yorkshire where the Scots also held a claim. After the death of his father, John decided to travel to the family's seat at Courcy in the Calvados region of Normandy. It was here that he learned his battle skills and, with dreams of conquering his own principality, he set his sights on Lecale, somewhere he would undoubtedly have known of beforehand since trade routes across the Irish Sea were easier than those to Somerset. He seized the opportunity to join the Anglo-Norman expedition to Dublin with the intention of bringing his renegade army to Uladh.

Cardinal Vivian, the papal legate sent by His Holiness Pope Alexander III to visit the churches in Scotland, Ireland, and Norway, was at that time the guest of Rory MacDunleve in Downpatrick. When the English overthrew the castle, the cardinal was left outdoors wearing only his night attire. Incensed by the attack on the honour of his father, Rory's son, Roderick, began to plan retaliation and so he gathered an army of ten thousand men to save Downpatrick from the hands of the English. When de Courcy heard of this, he challenged Roderick to battle. The odds looked to favour the Irish with a ratio of just four hundred Englishmen to ten thousand Irishmen. However, "nothing was heard on all sides, but tears, groans and lamentations, whilst the streams were dyed with the blood of the innocent inhabitants."[1] Remarkably the English had overcome their enemy due largely to the superiority of their weaponry and army training.

Afterwards the Most Rev. Malachy, Bishop of Down, was taken prisoner. It was Cardinal Vivian who pleaded the case to John de Courcy for Malachy to be restored to his dignities. Why though would someone who had been so terribly shamed by this warrior be willing to work with him? As it turned out the papal mission of Cardinal Vivian to Ireland was to hasten the island's subjugation to the English and assert the right of Henry II to the throne of Ireland. Contrary to the warlike and cruel nature which John de Courcy displayed, he was at the heart of it all a God-fearing man. He actually slept on a written copy of the prophecy of Saint Columba believing that the destruction of the province of Uladh applied to him.

In 1183 John de Courcy resolved that the Cathedral of the Holy Trinity, which was before then a monastery of secular canons, should be reconstituted. Its dedication was transferred to the Abbey of Saint Patrick and Benedictine monks from Chester were installed there with William Etleshale as their prior. The change of dedication was believed by many to have contributed to the

[1] Page 279, *A History of Ireland*.

downfall of John de Courcy. In spite of their differences Malachy, the Bishop of Down, accepted the role of abbot and endowed the church with several tracts of land. In addition to this, half of the offerings of the five great festivals, namely Christmas, Candlemas, Saint Patrick's Day, Easter, and Pentecost, were granted to it.

To pay penance for the blood spilt in the gaining of his new principality, as well as the destruction of the Abbey of Saint Finian at Erenagh which had fortified itself against him, the Abbey of Inch was enlarged by de Courcy. He rededicated it to the Blessed Virgin whom he surely hoped would intercede for him. The reformed abbey was given over to the Cistercian Order and remarkably no local person ever visited it before the Dissolution. Its inhabitants were always monks from Furness in Lancashire. This abbey, built in the 1180s, was one of the first to be erected in the new gothic style which had originated in France. The other early gothic abbey was that founded at Greyabbey by Affreca de Courcy, his wife.

Bishop Malachy was coerced by de Courcy to make it his mission to recover the remains of Saints Patrick, Brigid, and Columba which had been buried in the abbey yard at Downpatrick. The case seemed hopeless and Malachy was very much aggrieved by what seemed like a fruitless search. However, in 1185, whilst at prayer, he had his attention drawn to a particular spot where, when the earth was removed, the relics were found in a triple cave with Saint Patrick in the middle. Delegates were sent to inform His Holiness Pope Urban III. Cardinal Vivian returned to Downpatrick for the solemn translation of the relics on the feast of the venerated Saint Columba on 9 June 1186.

To ingratiate himself further with the people under his dominium de Courcy, with the consent of the Most Rev. Thomas O'Connor, Archbishop of Armagh, as well as Malachy, Bishop of Down, had Jocelin write the *Life of Saint Patrick* at Inch Abbey. Traditionally monks had always been persuaded by the English to take an interest in the success of the house of the local lord. For the first time in centuries Saint Patrick was restored to the hearts and minds of the Irish. This helped the provenance of the land held by the self-styled Prince of Ulster[2]. Downpatrick became a centre of pilgrimage not only for Ireland but also for continental Europe. To ensure that this holy place became a visit of note, the abbey was further endowed with several prebends in order to fund renovations and enlargements.

Of the army of four hundred which arrived in Lecale in January 1177, several grants of land were made to de Courcy's prominent accomplices. Many of these men bore witness to several acts created by John de Courcy and it has since been discovered that many of those signatories were childhood friends of his from Yorkshire. Without a doubt the man whose name is borne by part of this parish was long acquainted with John de Courcy. He was Rogerus de Dunesford, or if he were to come here today, Roger from Dunsforth in the West Riding of Yorkshire.

From the year 1194 the church at Dunsford's revenue was appropriate to the Abbey of Saint Patrick. The charter in Rogerus' own name states:

> Let it be known...that I Rogerus de Dunesford, with the knowledge and consent of my wife and my heir Thomas, have given to God and Saint Mary of York and to the monks of Nendrum there serving God, the Church of Anelor, with everything thereto pertaining and with one carucate of land, which lies between the wood and villa, and all other churches and gifts of churches from my entire land...except the free Church of Dunesford...for the well being of my lord, John de

---

[2] When de Courcy began to call himself Prince of Ulster this enraged the fickle tyrant King John. The warrant for his arrest was sent and he was taken back to England and imprisoned at the Tower of London in 1205, on the count of treason. The day he was arrested was Good Friday, a day when it was known that he would be unarmed and in the Abbey of Saint Patrick. Hugh de Lacy, the willing captor and Lord Justice of Ireland, was a long term rival of the de Courcy family. John de Courcy was such a warrior that he slew thirteen of de Lacy's army with a wooden cross, the nearest object he could find, before he was subdued.

Courcy, who gave me this land, for the well being of my wife and my heirs, and of all my predecessors and successors. In the year of Our Lord 1194 in the capital York, when I entered the society and order.

The name of part of this parish can almost certainly have taken on Rogerus' surname just in the same manner as in other parts of Lecale where we have Audley's Acre, Crolly's Quarter, Jordan's Acre, Russell's Quarter, Russell's Quarter North and Russell's Quarter South, lands which also appropriated money to the Abbey of Saint Patrick[3].

The Episcopal See

So far we have only examined one church in the area, the medieval Saint Mary's. Dunsford has always presented a conundrum and has long been a thorn in the side of the historian who has struggled to decipher where exactly the seat of the lord of the manor was. In many other parts of the barony of Lecale, it has been very easy to determine where the lord resided as they have left their tower-house castle or rath. The solution however can be found if you read at a glance with fresh eyes the names of some of the townlands in and around the parish – it was at Bishop's Court. In former days, this place was known as Lios Maolain[4] or Maolain's fort, clearly an early stronghold.

Why though would a bishop desire to reside six miles from his See House? The answer is rather simple. Dunsford is one of the most fertile areas in the whole of the Barony of Lecale. Where you have fertile ground you have the ability to create your own wealth.

---

[3] This Abbey's name was changed by John de Courcy and has since been returned to its original invocation of the Holy Trinity and better known to us today as Down Cathedral.
[4] Maolain, from the Gaeilge Maol meaning bald. Sometimes this word has an ecclesiastical usage to infer that the person is the servant of a clergyman or has dedicated his life to the work of a saint and usually signified by the person's tonsured head. Saint Malachy's name was, for example, actually Mael Maedac Ua Morgair.

The palace constructed here served as an administrative centre to the diocese and was complete with its own church, dedicated to Saint Malachy, and documented in the taxation of His Holiness Pope Nicholas IV[5] in the year 1291. A couple of centuries later it joined Dunsford as a prebend to the Abbey of Saint Patrick. The church appears to have survived, or at least the walls of it did, until after the Plantation. The bawn which was erected at Mountjoy Hill subsequent to the Reformation, had the chapel of Lios Maolain nearby. This is church number two.

The influence of the episcopal see is further demonstrated in the very peculiar parish boundaries which existed around Mountjoy Hill, the site of the bishop's court. Immediately adjoining this parish is the townland of Ballyorgan which is now part of the parish of Kilclief, but which was formerly a detached portion of the parish of Rathmullan. The church here, just eight fields away, was also under the invocation of Saint Mary, and up to the twentieth century the Magee family of 'the Hill' were custodians of certain black vessels, either pewter or silver, which it was believed belonged to the church. These were kept in the attic and were shown to Fr. Cross, a priest recuperating in Chapeltown. He suggested that they should be deposited in the National Museum of Ireland. He left the parish with these items and returned to the south of Ireland though it remains unclear if they were ever given to the museum as he said they should[6].

Travelling along the Crew Road towards Ardglass, you pass through the townland of Tollumgrange where there was another church, just a matter of twenty fields as the crow flies from Bishop's Court. The site is located at the crest of the hill a few fields away from the road. The vista from here is a rather impressive one,

---

[5] The valuation undertaken by His Holiness Pope Nicholas IV, who reigned as pope from 1288 to 1292, was primarily to fund the crusades, and, from this income, Edward I was granted one tenth for a period of six years.

[6] As told to the author by Kathleen Gill whose husband Martin held the fields around the site in conacre. Searches of the deposits made to the Museum have been unable to locate any record.

The Mourne mountains, as viewed from the site of the church of Tollumgrange.

overlooking Ardglass and Ardtole with the Mourne Mountains making a spectacular backdrop. The revenues generated here were granted to Greyabbey in the Ards. The rectory of Tollumgrange extended from here north to Ballybeg and Corbally, and east to Ballyedock and Sheepland Beg. John Casselles, the abbot of Greyabbey in 1538, held the rights and the tithes of Tollumgrange, Ballyedock, and Corbally. According to the inquisitions of the Montgomerys who were granted Greyabbey, the rights extended over Ballybeg and Sheepland Beg, but the tithes did not. Though today nothing remains of this site, it is understood that the rounded ballaun stone with the incised cross on the right hand side of the path at Chapeltown came from here.

Next within the parish and attached to Tollumgrange, is the townland of Ross which was formerly a detached portion of the parish of Kilclief. This site is just a matter of two fields away from the site of Tollumgrange church. Under the taxation of His Holiness Pope Nicholas IV, Capella de Ros, the fourth church in the modern parish's jurisdiction, was valued at 17s 4d with a marginal note inferring that Ross was in a union with Ardglass and Ardtole. In 1386 John Stiward, vicar of Ardee in County Louth, part of the Archdiocese of Armagh, exchanged his benefice with John Scrope, parson of the "free chapel of Rosse in the diocese of Down." In 1992 the environment agency paid a visit to the site with Desmond and Patrick Connor. They were able to point out the church path and a well which springs in winter, known as the Scrope Well, named after John.

In 1512, a little over a century after the exchange of Scrope and Stiward, the Most Rev. Tiberio Ugolino of Down and Connor annexed the chapel into the Prebend of Ross for the Abbey of Saint Patrick which was then in great need of repair. In 1518 the abbey was renewed[7] and, as part of the abbey's lands, this site too would have been visited by the king's surveyors less than twenty years later. By 1622 it was in a state of ruin, perhaps indicative of the fact that it was surplus to spiritual requirements. By the 1800s the site was wholly under tillage. No bones or other signs of a graveyard have ever been found and it is quite possible this site was more of an oratory.

At the same time in 1512 the rectory of Ardglass was also annexed to the Abbey of Saint Patrick by Bishop Tiberio. Reference to this church is made in the Registrum Johannis Mey where its title is styled "The Chapel of the Blessed Mary of Ardglass." In the registry of Primate Octavian de Palatio, a record is made that Marcus Omulynga resigned the rectory and Henery McKathmayll was appointed his successor in 1431. Seven years later the rector was Edward White.

Seated in the Chapel of the Blessed Mary was the ecclesiastical court. There is in the Vatican a fresco of a map of Ireland with

---

[7] According to a framed parchment from the cathedral recovered from a skip by Willie Mulhall.

only three ecclesiastical courts marked – Dublin, Armagh and, quite remarkably, Ardglass. It is because of the ecclesiastical court that the aforementioned churches are in procession towards the bishop's court.[8]

Also in this vicinity on the northern extremity of the parish at Killard was the church of Kenles. The site of this church can be found at a place called Cargy. It was valued at four marks under the taxation of Pope Nicholas IV. This same church was later found to be a chapel of the parish of Ballyculter with its tithes appropriate to the Abbey of Saul. These five churches, plus Saint Mary's in Ballyorgan, Dunsford, and Ardtole were all recorded in the taxation of Pope Nicholas in 1291. Their existence can be attributed to the reform of the church enacted by John de Courcy who had arrived in Lecale little more than a century earlier. They are, most certainly, more than even the current population of the area would require.

Right: Post Reformation memorial stone preserved at Saint Nicholas' Church of Ireland, Ardglass.

---

[8] With this knowledge the existence of the aforementioned churches becomes clear. They line the route from the ecclesiastic court of Ardglass to the bishop's court. This avenue, laid out to impress international delegates, follows the route from Ardtole along the Ballyedock Road, skirting the Crossmore Road, and joining the Crew Road at Ballybeg.

TWO
The Reformation

In 1536 George Browne had been appointed to the vacant Archbishopric of Dublin[9] by Henry VIII under the Act of Supremacy, thus overruling the Papacy. From Dublin Archbishop Browne was to set the foundations for the Reformation in Ireland. One of the first acts he carried out was to cause the burning of the Bachal Isu[10] which was preserved in Christ Church Cathedral in Dublin, as it was considered a superstitious relic. Ireland had disproportionately more abbeys than England, and to Henry VIII reformation was not so much about religious reform, but rather its main objective was the redistribution of the abbey lands and decimation of the wealth of the bishops[11]. The initial phase of the suppression of the monasteries, in 1537, legalised the closure of twelve monastic sites – Bective, Saint Peter's beside Trim, Duiske, Holmpatrick Dublin, Baltinglas, Grane, Taghmolin, Dunbrodie, Tintern, Ballybogane, Hogges and Fernes. In this list there is a glaringly obvious name missing – the Abbey of Saint Patrick.

There is a strong prevailing tradition that the suppression of this abbey was initiated by Lord Deputy Grey. So just who was Leonard Grey and did he really undertake this work? His grandmother was Queen Consort to Edward IV and his brother-in-law was Gerald, 9th Earl of Kildare. In 1536, he was raised in the peerage of Ireland as the 1st Viscount Grane. Accounts present

---

[9] The area around Dublin, known as The Pale, and Lecale were the places where English law was upheld. Armagh had been the Primatial See since the time of Saint Patrick. However, from the time of the appointment of Archbishop Browne until the incumbency of Archbishop Richard Robinson in the 1770s, Dublin claimed entitlement to be the Primatial See of the Anglican Church in Ireland.

[10] The Bachal Isu was the staff given by a hermit to Saint Patrick on an island in the Etruscan Sea. It was said to have been left there by Jesus with an instruction to give it to Patrick. It was enshrined by Saint Tassach of Raholp, and held at Christ Church from 1181, having been housed there by order of William FitzAdelm. It was greatly venerated by the Irish because whoever could lay claim to it, and the Gospels of Saint Patrick, was able to declare himself the legitimate Archbishop. John de Courcy gave Ballykinlar to fund a perpetual light before the relic. Its name translates into English as Jesus' staff.

[11] His Holiness Pope Julius III sent Cardinal Pole to England to reconcile the country to the Roman Catholic Church and to condone the confiscation of monastic property. On 30 November 1554, during the Council of Trent, the legate, by formal petition of both Houses of Parliament, absolved the country from heresy and schism.

him in a villainous light and it is claimed that he was so cruel that he ended the life of his elderly predecessor, William Skeffington. William had been Lord Deputy of Ireland up to 1535 when he died at the age of seventy. We know from a letter from Grey to Thomas Cromwell in 1539 that he "toke another castell, being in Mcgynons countre, called Doundrome, whych I assure your Lordeship, as yt standyth, ys one of the strongyst holtes that ever I sawe in Irelande, and moost comodios for the defence of the hole countre of Lecayll."[12] He had been in this area at the time on a mission to capture his thirteen year old nephew, Gerald FitzGerald, then the 11th Earl of Kildare.

When the Earl managed to escape from Ireland and make it to France in 1539, Lord Deputy Grey was arrested and charged with treason. When he was executed at the Tower of London in 1541, there was added to the count against him "that, without any warrant from the King or Counsaile, he prophaned the Church of Saint Patrickes in Doune, turning it into a stable, after he plucked it downe, and shipt the notable ring of belles that did hang in the Steple, meaning to have them sent to Englande, hadde not God of his justice prevented his iniquitie, by sinking the Vessell and passengers wherein the sayde Belles should have been conveyed."[13]

Concurrently, in 1539, the Most Rev. Robert Blyth, who had been Bishop of Down and Connor for nineteen years, accepted Royal Supremacy and, as a consequence, His Holiness Pope Paul III deposed him, appointing the Most Rev. Eugene Magennis as his replacement. Magennis himself accepted Royal Supremacy in 1541. Whether he did this discreetly or not he held on to the See of Down and Connor up to and throughout the reign of Mary I

---

[12] Translated as 'Took another castle, being in Magennis country, called Dundrum, which I assure your Lordship, as it stands, is one of the strongest holds that ever I saw in Ireland, and most commodious for the defence of the whole country of Lecale.'

[13] Translated as 'That, without any warrant from the King or Council, he profaned the Church of Saint Patrick's in Down, turning it into a stable, after he plucked it down, and shipped the notable ring of bells that did hang in the steeple, meaning to have them sent to England, had God not in his justice prevented his iniquity, by sinking the vessel and passengers wherein said bells should have been conveyed.'

who then began a Catholic restoration. Two years into the reign of Elizabeth I, the Act of Supremacy was once more enforced with the Book of Common Prayer prescribed. Eugene Magennis was later deposed in 1565. The third bishop of the See of Down and Connor, after 1536, was Miler Magrath who again accepted Royal Supremacy in 1567, and three years later accepted Elizabeth's offer of the Archbishopric of Cashel. It was another decade before His Holiness Pope Gregory XIII deposed him. According to the Rev. Monsignor Ambrose Macaulay, diocesan historian, "the confused situation is well illustrated by the fact that Miler's wife was accused of being a papist who frequently attended Mass."[14] And as well as this, these three bishops are recognised by the Roman Catholic diocese and are shared with the Anglican church as its first three bishops.

Exactly what was the reason for reform?

Looking back on these events of almost five hundred years ago, it is difficult to contemplate the need for reform without context. In Ireland "spiritual and moral abuses were common. Preaching was neglected so that the people were ignorant of their religion and given to superstition. Church services were carelessly performed and sometimes omitted altogether. Vocations to the priesthood dwindled and divine service had to be curtailed. Some religious communities had become so small that they gave up monastic life and sold off the abbey lands. Usually the abbot or prior kept the main buildings and the monks became no different from the lay people amongst whom they lived."[15]

Ordinary clergy were paid a very meagre salary and, as a result, they could not attend to the needs of the faithful properly because they had to support themselves by farming. This led in turn to an acceptance of priests falling into the habit of neglecting their vocational duties. Thus the priesthood attracted few men

---

[14] Page 29, *Down and Connor – A Short History*.
[15] Page 30, *Ireland Two*.

of ability and learning and impoverished dioceses often had no choice but to allow one man to hold several church positions, none of which received enough attention.

Once again bishops were in the habit of establishing dynasties. We don't have to look too far for a notorious example of a bishop who can be viewed as a secular lord as it happened in this vicinity at Bishop's Court. John Cely was a typical example of the pre-Reformation bishop. Having accumulated his wealth he built Kilclief Castle as a symbol of it in 1413. He was also cohabitating with his married housekeeper. For this he was unseated and took up the position of Prior of Down. At the time of John's deprivation in May 1441 a complaint was made which speaks of the essence of this tyranny. "John, as by virtewe of unyoune of our holy fader the Pope Bysshop of Down and Connoresse" was in a row with "Master Thomas Pollard pretending him through the Appostell provision for Bysshop of Down, undewly and with vyolence through help and power of his adherents in that parte entred his plaiss of Lesmolyn and noght only his godes there but of his rentes and divers and others his pertynaments hath spoyled and witholdes, &c."[16] John point blank refused to accept the decision of His Holiness Pope Eugene IV. Thomas, who was later in 1447 consecrated as bishop in Rome, only succeeded to the appointment in 1449 after the death of John Cely due to friction from the Primate Johannis Mey, a supporter of John. Thomas Pollard died shortly afterwards and when his successor Richard Wolsey resigned the See, the Diocese of Down and Connor was created in 1453. This strained further the resources yet increased the wealth appropriate to the bishop. The abuses within the ecclesiastical structure were not contested for well over another century. It was His Holiness Pope Pius IV

---

[16] Registrum Johannis Mey: extracted from *Ecclesiastic Antiquities of Down, Connor, and Dromore* (page 37) by William Reeves. Translated as 'Master Thomas Pollard pretending through the Apostle provision for the Bishop of Down, unduly and with violence through the help and power of his adherents in that part entered his Palace of Lios Maolain and not only his godes there but of his rents and divers and others his pertainments has spoiled and withholds'.

who tackled them. He reigned from 1559 to 1565 and successfully closed the Council of Trent.

What were the local effects of the Reformation?

Whilst it cannot be stated for certain who caused the destruction of the chapel at Dunsford, it is worth noting that at the enactment of the Dissolution, when Lord Deputy Grey came to Downpatrick, the Church's revenue was still appropriate to the aforementioned Abbey of Saint Patrick and worth £4 annually. Before the Dissolution of the monasteries commenced, a visitation and survey of the Abbey of Saint Patrick and its lands would have been undertaken. During this any observation of superstitious worship was documented. Obviously, when this survey was carried out, a visit to Dunsford would also have been necessary. Here the shrine of Our Lady of Dunsford, by then one of County Down's most famed sites, would have been recorded to become a target for eradication.

After 1583 the church was leased to Gerald FitzGerald, the 11th Earl of Kildare who had returned to England after the death of Henry VIII in 1547. Upon his return, he found favour at both the courts of Edward VI and subsequently Mary I who restored him to both his lands and titles. During his time in France, he studied at a monastery in Liège, developing, like others of the Renaissance era, an interest in alchemy and became known by the name of the Wizard Earl which aroused much suspicion to locals around Kilkea Castle in County Kildare. He was often accused of treason and sent to the Tower of London although Elizabeth I twice found favour in him and saved him from execution. He died in 1585 whilst under virtual arrest in London, and so perhaps Dunsford was thereby granted to him as a compensation for this hindrance.

Elizabeth I, who had come to the throne in 1558, was met with many obstacles to her authority in Ireland. Her main opponent to running a cheap government came from The O'Neill. This anarchy culminated in the Nine Years War, the effects of which were felt within this parish when the O'Neill sept besieged Jordan's Castle[17] for three years. Elizabeth I appointed Charles Blount, Lord Mountjoy, as successor to the Earl of Essex as Lord Deputy. A much more capable soldier, he quickly put an end to the hit and run tactics of the rebelling Irish. In 1601 he sailed with a fleet from Dublin and arrived at Ardglass on 17 June. He relieved the garrison and quickly drove off the besiegers into Dunsford where a battle was fought and the crown forces emerged victorious. During this period they had camped on Mountjoy Hill at Bishop's Court, thus giving the eminence its name. For his resistance against The O'Neill, Simon Jordan was awarded a concordat, a treaty recognising his position as a Catholic royalist.

The solution from Rome

Under the Counter Reformation the Pope, His Holiness Saint Pius V who reigned from 1566 to 1572, ensured that no diocese was left without leadership and, in cases where the appointment of a bishop might have incited retaliation, a priest could be given special powers, sometimes referred to as those of a Vicar Apostolic. Theology became a compulsory study but in Ireland it was not possible to found seminaries. The solution to this was found by using existing trading links with France and Spain, colleges were established in Lisbon, Valladolid, Salamanca, Paris, and Douai. Before travel, of course, it was necessary to learn Latin, which led to the development of the hedge schooling system. It was also illegal to travel with the intention of matriculating from any of these colleges but willing merchants were found to facilitate these journeys. Rome also gave permission for Mass to be celebrated in any place. The result of these measures was that, by 1600[18], Ireland

---

[17] A few written sources refer to the Jordans as the Palatine Barons of Dunsford, which may well be the reason that the Jordans held an acre for the Abbey of Saint Patrick. The location of their acre is at the junction of the Ardglass and Ballyhornan roads at Edward Street. Until the twentieth century this land was virtually undeveloped.

[18] During this period in 1588 the Bishop of Down and Connor, the Most Rev. Cornelius O'Devany, was incarcerated at Dublin Castle for almost three years. At this time,

was the only country in Europe where the Counter Reformation succeeded against the will of the sovereign.

Throughout the Counter Reformation, Lecale's importance never dwindled and it was home to two of the most important Elizabethan ports, Ardglass and Strangford. At Ardglass the Chapel of the Blessed Mary, now the site of Saint Nicholas' Church of Ireland in Kildare Street, appears to have been rebuilt[19]. In Strangford, Old Court Chapel was built by Valentine Payne in 1629. The latter was a place of worship for all denominations in its early days as all other ecclesiastical buildings nearby were in ruins. It remains unclear if Saint Nicholas' performed the same role.

For the Old English their position was secure as long as they could claim allegiance to Elizabeth I, whilst still remaining Catholic. This changed however, when His Holiness Saint Pius V excommunicated Elizabeth, declaring her a heretic, and inviting Catholic powers to depose her in 1570. From this date, the position of the Old English became more impossible. In the same year the Ward family arrived at Caraig na Sionnach[20]. They mingled well with the established Catholic landowners, and testament to this can be seen in the marriage of Elinor Russell to Nicholas Ward. Eventually however the government became hostile to the positions held by the Old English and, as a result, they forged ties with their Irish neighbours.

In 1609, under the Reformation settlement and according to the letters of James I, Saint Mary's Dunsford was raised to the head of the corps of the Prebend of Dunsport[21]. In the same year

---

prisoners were responsible for paying for their own upkeep but he managed to survive by convincing the prisoner below him to share his beer and bread with him through a crack in the floor.

[19] Preserved in the porch of Saint Nicholas' is one of the oldest headstones in Ulster which dates to 1585. It was uncovered at the time of the removal of the ruins in 1810 along with an ivory handled bell. Beneath the pulpit are the original flagstones of the medieval chapel's floor.

[20] Now known to us as Castle Ward.

[21] In Down Cathedral today, you can find the seat of the Prebendary of Dunsport in the stalls to the left of the entrance to the nave of the cathedral, although the position is an

James I had sanctioned an act for the restoration of the Abbey of Saint Patrick under its initial invocation of the Holy Trinity. His intention was obviously to restore the relationship between the two. James I, as monarch and head of the Anglican Church, was eager to reform the church and its teachings. His approved version of the Bible was completed between 1604 and 1611. The previous year in 1608, he had also granted a licence to Sir Thomas Phillipps establishing the Bushmills distillery – I have often heard it joked that he was perhaps in need of salvation for this! However, despite a succesion of prebendaries from 1609, these efforts in Dunsford appear to have lacked support. The church in 1622 was returned as a ruin by the Anglican Bishop. It was another one hundred and sixty seven years before any work was undertaken on the Cathedral of the Holy Trinity.

The Penal era

In June 1611 the Most Rev. Blessed Cornelius O'Devany was recaptured while performing a confirmation. This time he was held on the charge of aiding Hugh O'Neill's escape to the continent four years previously. Three times he refused to take the Oath of Supremacy and was thus found guilty of treason. He was sentenced to be hanged and cut down, to have his entails drawn out while still alive, and for his body to be quartered. He went to his martyrdom in his eightieth year on Saint Brigid's Day 1612 at the same time as Blessed Patrick O'Loughran[22]. Their executioner was a robber who gained release for the deed; no Irishman would undertake the gruesome task. His successor to the See, the Most Rev. Edmund Dungan, after enduring severe hardships, died in chains while incarcerated at Dublin Castle on 2 November 1628.

The Catholic Church carried on with its efforts but, under the Commonwealth of Cromwell, Catholicism was banned and the

---

extinct one.
[22] Both the Most Rev. Cornelius O'Devany and the Rev. Fr. Patrick O'Loughran were beatified along with other Irish martyrs in 1992.

number of priests dwindled. After the Lord Protector's son was deemed unfit to govern a republic Charles II was instated to the throne and the Restoration began. Whilst he was kindly towards the Catholic faith, he only converted on his deathbed. During his reign there was reorganisation of the Catholic church and, under a new policy of ordaining men with little or no training, the number of clergy had reached sixteen hundred by the time Saint Oliver Plunket was appointed to the Archbishopric of Armagh in 1669.

During the Church of Ireland's first century in Ulster, the view of the reformed congregation was much more aligned towards Puritanal aspects. Catholicism was viewed very much as idolatry driven by superstition. And so, by taking this viewpoint, the Church of Ireland was willing to tolerate having Presbyterian ministers at the head of parishes. This continued until the incumbency of Bishop Jeremy Taylor (1660-1667) in Down and Connor when he sacked no less than twenty nine Presbyterian ministers, some of whom, even despite their loss of income, continued to preach.

In 1673, anti-Catholic laws were enforced once again. Later, when Titus Oates concocted the lie of the Popish Plot, Catholic clergy were ordered to leave the country with hostility towards them once again heightened. There were a few people willing to conceal priests, but for any landowner to do so was a precarious act. In October 1690, at a session of the County Down Assizes in the Grand Jury Room, Downpatrick, Jocelyn Hamilton was accused by his cousin Bernard Ward, then High Sheriff of County Down, of helping a priest to escape. The story goes that the priest was brought as a prisoner to Hamilton's home. Before morning, a Catholic servant was told to saddle the best horse. The plan was to assist the priest to escape to the house of a Mr Savage at Drumaroad. In his role, Bernard Ward would have made it his duty to arrange for the exile of all the Catholic clergy. This accusation resulted in a furious quarrel erupting with the two men then proceeding to fight a duel beneath the ruins of the Abbey of Saint Patrick where the Southwell School now stands. From all accounts the duel "was conducted in the most irregular fashion. The High Sheriff mortally wounded his opponent with a pistol. As Jocelyn was shot he cried out, 'Foul stroke, Cousin Ward', leaping forward and, in retaliation, he made a thrust with his sword with which he managed to kill his opponent that he was run "through almost to the hilt."[23]

Under William and Mary, a Banishment Act was put in place in 1697. The particulars of this document meant that each parish was allowed one priest who could not be replaced at the event of his death. Furthermore, no priest was allowed to return to the country from the continent and bishops were exiled which meant new priests could not be ordained. As with many laws, however, loopholes were found and provided that they did it discretely, bishops were allowed to register as parish priests. In 1704 the Act of Registration was created to appease ill feeling from Catholic powers on the continent who were concerned by the repression of the faith. The act, for the first time in almost two centuries, enabled the priest to officiate openly in their parishes with legal recognition to do so. It was for this reason that we have a record of the first priests since the Reformation. In Dunsford we have the Rev. Fr. Daniel Lea[24] returning as parish priest. He was ordained by Oliver Plunket in 1670. At the same time, thirty seven year old Rev. Fr. James McGee, who resided at Ballyorgan, was returned as Parish Priest at Ardglass. It appears that both were separate parishes, much in the same way as with the Established Church.

While this situation may appear more uplifting, there was much disruption to the See up to the year 1711 with Vicars General and Vicars Apostolic holding power over the separated Diocese of Down and Connor. The Most Rev. James O'Shiel was the first bishop appointed to the reunified diocese in over sixty years in 1717.

Both of the aforementioned priests were followed, in oral

---

[23] From an Introduction to the Ward Papers held at PRONI and from Maurice Hayes historical book on Killough, *The Church on the Lough*.

[24] An early form of the surname McAlea.

tradition, by a Rev. Fr. Hanna of the united parish of Dunsford and Ardglass. Of Fr. Hanna this is all that is known, as discretion was still required. Next came the Rev. Fr. John Teggart, a native of Ballywalter, who held this parish in conjunction with Ballee and Kilclief. The Rev. Fr. William Megarry[25] took over Dunsford and Ardglass in 1742 remaining in this role until his death in 1763. He was born in Crossmore and resided at Ballyedock, appearing to be the first priest to reside in the parish since the Banishment Act. He also was able to have a curate, the Rev. Fr. Daniel O'Doran[26], who was appointed Parish Priest upon Fr. Megarry's death. Fr. O'Doran remained in the parish until 1766.

The following is a transcription of a letter to the House of Lords from a minister of the Church of Ireland which supports these traditions:

Killough, April 12, 1766.

Sir in the parish of Dunsport three score and fourteen Protestant families, six score and sixteen Papists; and in the adjoining parish of Ardglass there are twenty-nine Protestant families and sixty-two Papists. There is no Popish priest or friar residing in either parish, but they are served in the meanwhile by two neighbouring priests till a supply be for it. I would have sent this account before, but have been so unwell that I was unable – I am, sir your most obedient and very humble servant.

Wynne Stewart.

To Robert Sterne, Esq., Clerk to the Honourable House of Lords.[27]

---

[25] Further information on the Rev. Fr. William Megarry can be found in chapter 9 – 'Vocations from the Parish'.
[26] Further information on the Rev. Fr. Daniel O'Doran can be found in chapter 9 – 'Vocations from the Parish'.
[27] Page 183, An Historical Account of the Diocese of Down and Connor, Volume 1.

The remarkable Edward Smyth

After the Rev. Fr. O'Doran left for Ards, it was the duty of the Rev. Fr. William McAlea, Parish Priest of Ballee, to minister in Dunsford and Ardglass. As well as this he was responsible for Kilclief. He held these duties from 1766 until he resigned them after eight years in 1774. It was about this time that Methodism became prominent in Dunsford as the Ordnance Survey Memoirs tell:

> The Methodists were once numerous in this parish, which is remarkably connected with the rise and progress of that sect, as it was at a place called Ringawiddy they held their first meeting, from whence their meetings and principles and mode of worship were diffused over the country. At that period and for some years after, the minds of the people were kept in a state of continual agitation by the supposed miracles performed, the appearances of angels, visions, etc.; people falling into swoons and some into fits. Their numbers are on the decrease, their zeal much abated and the extravagances cited above have entirely ceased.

John Wesley had made his first visit to Ireland in 1747 as an Anglican minister. Methodism was a movement within the Anglican Church until the point when it broke away in 1783. When John Wesley came to Dunsford, he preached in the field next to the medieval church. It is noted in his journal that he did so on Sunday 14 June 1778. A tireless and charismatic preacher, Wesley averaged about eight thousand miles per year on horseback, giving sermons across Great Britain and Ireland. It is believed that he stayed at Rourke's house at Ringawaddy having been invited to Dunsford by the Rev. Edward Smyth[28]. Smyth had been sacked

---

[28] The Rev. Edward Smyth was the nephew of the Archbishop of Dublin, and his appointment to Ballyculter was considered at the time as rather prestigious.

from Ballyculter by Bernard Ward, the first Lord Bangor, after he became the subject of a sermon publicly rebuking him. Smyth had witnessed an extra marital dalliance with a housemaid, and felt it his place to admonish Bernard. The insulted Lord Bangor petitioned Bishop Trail. His Lordship and the bishop took him to court, on a charge of practising Methodism. They forcibly removed him and the congregation from Christ Church in Ballyculter shortly afterwards. Undeterred by the events, the Rev. Smyth continued the service outside in exile in the rain but was saved from the downpour by a gentleman by the name of Greer who held up an umbrella for him. The family has a saying 'The luck of the Greers'[29] on account of their good fortune ever since this event.

Methodism won the people over through its activism and it was at a meeting at Derriaghy that the Rev. Edward Smyth met Ireland's first woman preacher, Margaret Davidson. In 1776, at his insistence, she was coerced to speak to the people at Dunsford. Persuaded to stay, flocks of people came to listen to this blind preacher and, within a month, no fewer than one hundred people had encountered a powerful spiritual awakening. This is clearly what the Ordnance Survey Memoirs are alluding to.

Without a church over which to preside, the Rev. Smyth went on to build himself a meeting house in Downpatrick, the one at the corner of Scotch Street and Saul Street. This he founded in 1777. Evidently the Rev. Smyth was always aware that this would be the destiny of the movement and it is held in regard that he was almost solely responsible for encouraging John Wesley to break from the Established Church. The rise of Methodism was clearly something which was a worry and strain to the resources of the priest as he, the Rev. Fr. William McAlea, resigned the administration of this parish and Kilclief. The effects of this also brought about the cessation of Stations of the Cross at Crossmore around this time.

---

[29] As told to the author by Mabel McComiskey, a descendent of the Greer family.

The Rev. Fr. Daniel Clinton[30], a native of Sheepland, was then appointed to the parish of Dunsford and Ardglass and acted as administrator to Kilclief. He carried on in this role until his death at the age of seventy seven in 1788. His successor as Parish Priest of Dunsford and Ardglass was the Rev. Fr. Edward Mulholland who arrived in the parish in the following year.

---

[30] Further details on the Rev. Fr. Daniel Clinton can be found in chapter 9 of 'Vocations from the Parish'.

The view east from the quarry field in Dunsford.

Saint Patrick's Well today.

THREE

The building of Chapeltown

Amid all the turmoil, a unique style of country life began to emerge from the relaxation of the Penal Laws. Lecale, as one of the richer areas in Ireland, became one of the first places where Masshouses were erected. Throughout Ireland there are around four hundred chapel villages which are the product of the new Catholic parish system. Normally built at crossroads the Masshouse was soon surrounded by the public house, school, post office, barracks, dispensary, and shops. Usually their formation was a wholly organic indigenous conception. As the *Atlas of the Irish Rural Landscape* describes them they have the appearance of a haphazard straggle.

Situated on the border of the townlands of Sheepland and Ballyedock is one of these "diffuse, haphazard straggles," the hamlet of Chapeltown. It was founded two hundred and twenty five years ago, in 1791, when the Rev. Fr. Edward Mulholland, a native of Loughinisland, began the erection of the new chapel for the Parish of Dunsford and Ardglass. It is very easy to imagine the reason that the five roads which converge at this point is due to the erection of the chapel. But going back to the mapping of the Earl of Kildare's Manor of Ardglass, surveyed in 1768, we can see that the roads meet in much the same way today as they did then. The amazing exception is that there were no buildings at the junction at all. The reason for the meeting of the five roads can still be viewed today at the former weighbridge. This was the junction to the Sheepland mills where local farmers came to have their corn ground.

Up to, and throughout the eighteenth century, the Lecale peninsula was a vast corn-growing region and at Dunsford, in particular, there were no farms exclusively devoted to grazing. At the time when this chapel was built, the local Anglican minister, the Rev. Samuel Burdy, known as Parson Burdy of Ardglass, wrote a book of poetry and historical notes published in 1802 entitled *Ardglass or the Ruined Castles*. In this work he writes of the region:

And hear the lofty billows roar,
And loud assail the sounding shore,
The shore that guards the fruitful vale,
And golden harvests of Lecale.

In 1790, when the Earl of Kildare's son, Rear Admiral Lord Charles James FitzGerald, came to reside in his newly constructed pile, Ardglass Castle, one of the first acts he undertook was to provide the Catholic parish with a site for their place of worship. When he arrived at Ardglass, it was no more than a cluster of rudimentary cabins nestled among the ruins of what was once Ireland's most fortified town, with six fortifications within one mile[31]. The ideal site was at the junction to the Sheepland mills where the congregation had already been meeting.

It is remarkable that the gift of the site by Lord Charles predates any church at that time at Ardglass or even at Dunsford for that matter. Saint Nicholas' Church of Ireland was only then under construction at the time of his death in 1810, and even his minister, Parson Burdy, would have had no church in which to preach. Charles instead chose to be interred, alongside his first wife, at the Manor of Ardglass' only Church of Ireland at Bright where a bust of him adorns the walls[32]. The medieval church site at Dunsford, which was later rebuilt in the 1790s, then belonged to Robert Hamilton Smyth who lived in Dunsford Park but it would not have been, of course, too pleasing for one landlord to be buried in the church of another.

The place for salvation

When the chapel was under construction, the Rev. Fr. Edward Mulholland made a conscious effort to gather up

---

[31] During the Confederate Wars of the 1640s Ardglass came under the control of the Irish and the English forces withdrew from the town. Eventually the wealth of the town and its significance diminished. By the 1700s the town had all but disappeared with the ruins of its castles remnants of its former glory.

[32] That church site is one of the oldest in Ireland and is accepted as Saint Patrick's second.

objects of antiquity from the medieval era. Visiting the different ecclesiastical establishments which were within the boundaries of the modern parish he gathered numerous artefacts. As you come up the path, you will pass on the left a large square ballaun stone of Scrabo sandstone which was brought from the medieval parish site half a mile away; this was used as a baptismal font there. Some of the older members of the congregation would still refer to this as the 'wart stone' as the water it holds possesses the capability of getting rid of unsightly warts. Opposite this ballaun stone, and on the right hand side of the pathway, is a cruder stone which was also used as a font originating from the church at Tollumgrange.

Situated above the porch door is an early Christian cross slab which was inscribed in the tenth century and flanked by the letters J and M on either side. This cross was most likely a grave marker and was brought from the ruins of Ardtole Church which we will explore later. Completing the collection of the relics of the parish's old places of worship was the head of Our Lady of Dunsford which Fr. Mullholland had located in the burial ground of the medieval parish church. When first constructed the chapel was a plain building, known as a barn chapel type, and adorned only with these relics.

Saint Mary's photographed by John MacMahon after the restoration of the shrine of Our Lady of Dunsford in 1908.

The place for damnation

At the side of the road opposite the chapel is Curran's Bar which was also constructed at the same time in 1791 . The existence of this establishment complements parochial events as it provides the ideal place to gather and celebrate the welcoming of a new member to the congregation after baptism, the place to toast the new bride and groom on the occasion of their marriage, and the place to lament the loss of a loved one. Throughout its long history this building has also witnessed many local municipal functions. The doctor would hold surgeries here after Mass on Sunday, people would come from far and wide to have their last will and testament written, and unwed local people would come to meet the matchmaker[33]. Curran's Bar, in the late nineteenth

[33] Until the early years of the twentieth century, marriages would be arranged with the older bachelors often having preference over the younger bachelors for the younger spinsters. It was also customary, after marriage, for the bride and her groom to continue to reside with their respective parents for a period of up to one month before a celebration called the 'hauling home'. On this salubrious occasion, people would come

century, would often play host to the Most Rev. Patrick McAlister who gave his name to the 'Bishop's Room' which is now part of the main bar. This however is not as unusual as it sounds as he was the cousin of the then owner, Ellen Smith.

The place for education

The National School system was a means of providing all the children of Ireland with a basic education. Prior to the introduction of this system, the predominant method was through hedge schooling and Dunsford, in the 1700s, had an excellent hedge school "in which boys were taught the Latin and Greek languages and instructed in the higher branches of mathematics."[34] In spite of the rudimentary provision of a hedge for a windbreak, several scholars went on to pursue noteworthy professions.

The main informant for the Lecale area to John O'Donovan who was responsible for recording the Ordnance Survey Memoirs, was a native of the parish, Dr William Hamilton Smyth. He noted that in the 1830s "the taste for classical learning [was] rapidly on the decline" and the school in which he received his learning had long since gone. The only replacements were two schools connected with the National Board of Education in which the pupils "are taught reading, writing and a few rules of arithmetic, the course of instruction not extending farther." The first school in the parish to be recognised was in Seahornan which belonged to Dan Murnin, an exceedingly talented instructor who had his establishment accepted on 13 September 1832.

---

and take the bride to her husband's house to reside. One of the shanties sung by the crowd in the procession was 'Óró, sé do bheatha abhaile'. Another point worth noting is that, whilst this was the traditional way, there were other means of procuring a marriage for oneself. Often these were twilight weddings where the bride and groom would call at the priest's house, with a few witnesses, or invite the priest to the house of a witness. The ceremony was performed with the oral consent of the bride's father. There have been a few occasions recorded in this parish when the disgruntled father would turn up at the door, shotgun in hand.

[34] Taken from the Ordnance Survey Memoirs, inserted by Dr. William Hamilton Smyth.

A sampler created by Ellen Fitzsimons at the National School.

The Board of Education was subject to the whims of the clergy of all denominations[35] and in Dunsford the rector, the Rev. Robert Rowan, sent a letter to the board in 1837 regarding

---

[35] There was another earlier National School in the civil parish of Dunsford which was a non-denominational Protestant school next to the Church of Ireland. The Rev. Dr. William Crolly, who himself had received education at the Rev. Neilson's Presbyterian school and at Mr. Doran's Catholic academy in Downpatrick, celebrated the successes of the national system's first decade: "Amongst the reasons assigned for allowing Catholics to avail of the advantages afforded by the national schools, are, the *opportunity* they will give for the instruction of youth – *gratitude* to parliament for granting large sums of money to schools for the Irish people – *the fear lest all the money and influence* should pass into the hand of heterodox teachers – and lastly that during the ten years in which that system was received, the Catholic religion had suffered no injury.'"

the length of the school day and religious instruction. The Board decreed that only the last hour of the school day should be devoted to this activity. Problems in the early years were compounded by this sort of issue and it is easy to see why it was resolved that separate Protestant and Catholic schools ought to be established. This was ultimately the project's biggest failure as there was a great degree of contention over the spiritual instruction of pupils. Thus, it was agreed, in 1841, that the hamlet should be endowed with a National School built on ground given by Major Aubrey William Beauclerk from land on James Smyth's farm. This said, throughout its lifetime the National School in Dunsford has always had an intake of pupils from other Christian denominations.

The school was replaced by a modern and better-equipped school which was opened on 23 May 1960 after a blessing by the Ven. Archdeacon David J. McWilliams of Downpatrick, who had served his time in Dunsford as a curate between 1897 and 1899. At the time of George Rice's writing in 1991, he anticipated that the school would face inevitable closure. Fortune, however, has shone on the establishment and it has, in my lifetime, undergone a revival under the leadership of John Magee.

The place for communication

In the *Atlas to the Irish Rural Landscape* it is noted that where the new chapels are constructed on so-called virgin sites, new settlements tended to spring up and, as evidenced thus far, this is true for Chapeltown. Supplementary to this there were local amenities and Chapeltown did indeed once have its own post office which closed in the early years of the present century. The Magee family ran the post office and shop for many years until it moved and, in its latter years, it was run by Margaret Gilchrist. At the heart of the post office's mission was the ability always to remain up to date with communication technology and this was provided by the means of a K12 telephone box. The Magees also had a bit of healthy competition from the Byrne family who ran a shop from their home at number one Church Road.

In addition to these two shops there were other services to be found in the hamlet. In the words of John Gordon, grandson and namesake of the last owner, "The blacksmith's shop was also an important meeting place for farmers to discuss the price of cattle, wheat, barley and other crops as well as picking up the local gossip. It being a warm environment because of the forge itself also made it an appealing place to be on a cold wet day."[36] The smithy was located on the green at the end of the Tollumgrange Road. If use of the wart stone didn't rid you of your disfigurement, you could always pay a visit to the blacksmith and ask him for some water from his tempering trough.

The forge was established here in the latter half of the nineteenth century and, for many years, it was run by the Gordon family. The blacksmith was the centre of country life for many of the people of the area as he was the person who would shoe your horse, mend your plough, and repair your wheels, and in fact anything that moved was essentially within the jurisdiction of a blacksmith's repertoire. The business survived until 1961 when John Gordon retired. John was assisted by Dan Shields who was responsible for ringing the Angelus. The two men had very contrasting temperaments, John being a joker and Dan taking a lot of what he would say literally without questioning it. The peal of the bell at Chapeltown can be heard for miles around and each day John would remark that Dan should, 'Go and ring the bell so that the good men in the fields will know to come in for their tea'. Dan would always reply, 'Sure John, you should know that's not why I ring it!'

The corn mills mentioned previously also survived well into the twentieth century. They were run by the Curran family who originally rented them from the landlord. In 1710 Edward Southwell sold the townland of Sheepland Beg. He had come

---

[36] Page 13, *A Harvest of History*, Volume 1.

Chapeltown as it appeared in the 1950s. Photograph courtesy of John Gordon.

into possession of it through his wife Lady Elizabeth Cromwell who, proud of her heritage and bringing Downpatrick as part of her dowry, never took his name and held her own wealth which was unusual for a woman of her era. Her ancestors, the Earls of Ardglass, had petitioned the Crown to raise the lands of the Abbey of Saint Patrick into the Manor of Downpatrick. With the sale complete the new landlord, Sir Hector McNeill, the son of the Rev. Archibald McNeill, ensured that the revenue of the mills could be increased and built the windmill in and around 1730, making it one of the earliest in the area. It is worth noting that Lecale and the Ards once boasted claim to the largest concentration of windmills in Ireland. Today in most, but not all, cases[37] only their stumps remain.

Indeed, if you pass the stream which supplied the water to the mill even after a period of rain, you will notice that the flow

---

[37] Ballycopeland Windmill remains, to this day, in an excellent state of preservation.

of water is even then still not great. The millers worked hard to eke out a living for themselves but it was seasonal work for three months at ten hours per day. In addition to this, the land on which both mills were sited was poor and yielded few crops. Remarkably, at the time of the Tithe Applotments in the 1830s and the Griffiths Valuation in the 1860s the mills were worked by widows. Unlike others in the area, Sheepland's were never upgraded to process flax and contribute to local linen manufacturing even though there was a great deal of it carried out in the parish around 1810. In spite of their hardworking nature and the short working season during the Great Famine in 1847 the miller was fined half a crown for working the mills on the Sabbath. To equate this to its cost value then, it would have required the same amount of money to construct a round stone pillar. The mills continued up to the middle part of the twentieth century, and a large part of their demise can be attributed to the army who arrived with a lot of new agricultural machinery which they left behind at the end of the Second World War. A lasting reminder of the millers is the chalice used in Saint Mary's which was the gift of Patrick Curran in 1909, inscribed in both Latin and Gaeilge.

Jordan's Castle from the quayside.

A town once noted, of an ancient name
And well deserving of poetic fame.
Five castles here with ancient moss adorned,
Jordan's, King's, Margaret's, the Cow'd, and Horn'd

Parson Burdy, Ardglass or the Ruined Castles.

FOUR
Building the second chapel

Before the erection of Saint Nicholas' mass was celebrated, and stations and confessions were held, in the house of William Rooney in the town of Ardglass. With the house thronged to suffocation, the remainder of those gathered knelt outside the door and on the street. This house was the favourite station of the Rev. Fr. Eugene Mulholland. At the time of his arrival in the parish there was no town to minister to as the following paragraph will reveal.

It is easy to think of the 1920s as the decade of extravagance, but for the parish of Dunsford and Ardglass the Roaring Twenties occurred in the nineteenth century. Having bankrupted himself before his death on a mission to pursue a political career and after suffering the loss of his only son and heir Rear Admiral Lord Charles James FitzGerald, who had been raised in the peerage to Baron Lecale in 1801, was forced to sell the Manor of Ardglass in 1806 to his stepfather Mr William Ogilvie. It was indeed an odd arrangement which still allowed Baron Lecale to hold on to his baronial seat whilst developments were steered by Mr Ogilvie. Under his stewardship and capable business acumen, Ardglass flourished with the first project being the construction of the harbour which opened in 1813. It was the revenue from the harbour which funded the erection of the Georgian town which, due to its position on the eastern sea board and the purity of the water and air, soon made Ardglass the most desirable summer residence in the north of Ireland.

In 1828, the year preceding Catholic Emancipation, a suitable piece of land in High Street was granted free by Mr Ogilvie for the erection of Saint Nicholas' chapel. The land was granted to the curate, the Rev. Fr. John O'Heggarty, who negotiated with Mr Ogilvie. This was the second church to be built in the town with the Presbyterian and Methodist establishments being constructed later in the 1840s. The foundation stone was laid on May 29th. *Finns Leinster Journal* of Wednesday 11 June 1828 reported:

A happy parish

Ardglass May 29th – The first stone of the New Catholic Chapel of Ardglass was laid, on Monday last, on a plot of ground, granted for ever, free of rent, by William Ogilvie Esq. to the Roman Catholic inhabitants of Ardglass and its vicinity. On this interesting occasion we had the pleasure of witnessing a large and very respectable concourse of people, of all classes and creeds, assembled on the spot on which the sacred edifice is about to be raised. Amongst the dense crowd we beheld the Hon. and Very Rev. Dean Knox; the Rev. Mr. O'Neil, Rector, and son-in-law to the Dean; the Rev. John Hagarty; Captain Saunders; Henry Pentland, Esq., Doctor Nelson, &c. Nothing could exceed the cordial feelings evinced by every class of the community. Captain Saunders having, with the usual ceremony, laid the first stone, (unto which he deposited a very large donation to be appropriated to the interest of the house,) the vast multitude, with one simultaneous impulse, continued for a length of time to rend the air with loud and repeated huzzas. Shortly after, the more respectable, linked hand in hand in the social bond of fellowship, departed to spend together the festive evening. We are proud to state, that here no party feelings exist – here no man is known but by his virtues – here we shall continue to enjoy the blessings of the Constitution as long as we are blessed with such exemplary spiritual guides, and with such an upright, impartial Magistracy as we at present fortunately do possess.

The erection of the building was energised by Fr. O'Heggarty with the chapel consecrated just under six months later on 24 November by the Most Rev. Dr. William Crolly who was then the Bishop of Down and Connor. He preached afterwards to the assembled crowd about the charity and good feeling among all denominations of Christians. Again, in attendance, at the consecration were stood side-by-side Catholic, Protestant, and Dissenter. Included among the assembly who had donated and contributed towards the building were Mr William Ogilvie and Mr Knox, son of The Honourable Dean of Down. The sum collected on the occasion of the consecration amounted to £51.7s.6d.

In the evening the party sat down to a dinner in The Ardglass Arms, then one of Ulster's premier hotels. Dr. Crolly presided over the proceedings at dinner and was joined by Major Aubrey William Beauclerk, Mr. Ogilvie's grandson and heir; Captain Saunders, agent to Mr Ogilvie; Edmund Knox, Esq.; Henry Pentland, Esq.; C.G. Coslett, Esq.; Dr. William Hamilton Smyth; and many more respectable gentlemen.

As you may have already observed, the 1820s were filled with religious tolerance and Dr. Crolly, a native of Ballykilbeg in Lecale, would state that, "Should there be any priest tainted by narrow and gross prejudice I shall send them for his cure to inhale the liberal atmosphere of Belfast." Society in this part of the country was just as liberal and, from the diary of Richard Clark, it is quite evident that both Saint Nicholas' Church of Ireland and Ardglass Presbyterian Church were open to visits from all denominations on various occasions. Some of the occasions recorded include the first confirmation in Saint Nicholas' by Bishop Knox (formerly the Dean of Down) and the development of the Oxford Movement[38] under the Rev. Charles Campbell, in the Anglican church; and the laying of the foundation stone of the Presbyterian Church and the ordination of the Rev. McAfee, their minister for sixty years. By this time, it appears that the early zeal for Methodism in this area

---

[38] Richard Clark in his random notes records: "Oxford with 5 Professors of Protestant Theology has in 3 years made 23 of her members converts to Popery. 1845." In 1845 the Rev. Campbell, along with the Rev. Gordon of Ballyculter, placed a notice in the *Down Recorder* to abandon the Tractarian system which they had been following for three years. In essence this brought to an end the next form of reformation.

had waned and there only remained a small congregation usually of maritime employees or holidaymakers.

On the completion of Saint Nicholas', the importance of the parish's first chapel, Saint Mary's, began to diminish and it gradually became its secondary church. Before the death of Mr Ogilvie, at the ripe old age of 92 in 1832, he had successfully schooled his heir, Aubrey, in how the running of the estate should be carried on and, due to his foresight, Ardglass continued to grow in importance. Major Beauclerk, who like his grandfather appreciated and cared for the spiritual needs of his tenantry, donated funds, in 1850, for improving and furnishing Saint Nicholas' as the following letter which appeared in the *Down Recorder* evidences:

PROTESTANT LIBERALITY
To the editor of the Downpatrick Recorder.

Ardglass, January 9th, 1851,

Sir,

I take the liberty that you will allow me to acknowledge in the columns of your paper the receipt of £10 sterling from Major Beauclerk of Ardglass as a donation to assist in furnishing and improving the Catholic Church of this town and also to publish my gratitude and that of the Catholic Parishioners for this generous gift. This too is only one of a series of favours conferred by the same high minded individual on his Catholic Tenantry in this neighbourhood. They received from him many handsome subscriptions previously to this for the same church, and also a free grant of ground on which the church is built. Such deeds of generosity and liberality like the aims of Cornelius are generally the messengers of more abundant and valuable graces.

Your obedient servant,

W. MacMullan P.P.

It seems evident that when the chapel was originally constructed, it also bore a resemblance to the floor plan at Dunsford. The altar was sited along the rear north wall and it was noted that when Patt Kelly erected the confessional on Saturday 11 June 1852, it was positioned in the east corner which would be where the altar is located today. While the support of Major Beauclerk may not have come as a surprise, it was indeed remarkable, as he had also contributed to the Catholic chapel at Rossglass. The reader may be even more surprised to learn that, at this time, Saint Nicholas' Church of Ireland stood without a spire having lost its wooden one in a thunderstorm on 30 October 1848 and during this meteorological tempest the roof had also been damaged. Rather than foot the bill for its repair, Major Beauclerk left it to the Board of First Fruits which did not undertake its rebuilding until 1852.

The typical view of an absentee landlord was that of a miserly and unfeeling individual with a stranglehold over his tenantry but Major Aubrey William Beauclerk's reputation would clearly disagree with this sentiment and would contradict it at every turn. As a Chartist politician from Sussex, he campaigned, as a revolutionary, for the abolition of slavery and the discontinuation of tithes which, at that time, were in place to fund the Established Church. His personal life was rather colourful though, for his one known mistress was the author of *Frankenstein*, Mary Shelley, a neighbour of his in Sussex. His liberal generosity had in the past put Major Beauclerk under the scrutiny of Bishop Knox who publically rebuked him in the local and national press.

In his own words in 1842 to the Rev. Fr. John McKenna, Parish Priest of Bright, Major Beauclerk stated:

I shall be proud and happy to contribute towards it [walling in the new graveyard at Rossglass which he had given for free] as the head of your parishioners one of whom you will allow me to consider myself, for though fate may have embarked us on different routes (as regards our opinions) yet I feel convinced we aim (I most inefficiently) to reach the same happy port, and one of my doctrines is, to respect the sincere opinions of others and believe them actuated by the same motives as myself.

On his death at Ardglass Castle in 1854, at the age of 54, his loss was greatly lamented. The sense of mourning was further compounded by the fact that his son and heir, Aubrey de Vere Beauclerk, was the complete opposite of his father. Major Beauclerk's obituary in the *Down Recorder* reads:

In him the blood of the Norman Beauclerk mingled with the Irish Geraldine and the spirit of both was manifest in him through all the relation in life. Though by birth an Englishman, Major Beauclerk was an Irishman at heart; he was devotedly attached to the interests of Ireland, and whether in or out of Parliament, he never omitted an opportunity of saying a kind word of the country of his adoption.

After the death of Major Beauclerk, Ardglass began to suffer as his heir, Aubrey de Vere Beauclerk, was far more interested in enjoying the fortune he had inherited from his great grandfather, Mr Ogilvie. However, his debts eventually caught up with him and he filed for bankruptcy in 1906 resulting in the Ardglass estate going up in lots for auction in 1911. Both chapels now had to rely on making their own way through the kindness of their parishioners and endowments from the diocese.

A view of the parish from Killard Point.

Luke's Port in Ardglass where the bishops would have arrived to attend the ecclesiastic court.

ST. MARY'S,
DUNSFORD,
ARDGLASS,
CO. DOWN.

22nd. June 1961

Dear *John + Henry*,

The last undertaking by the farmers of the parish to rear cattle for parochial funds was a most successful one, and the priests and the people are most indebted to them for their generous response to the appeal of a few years ago.

It is now proposed to start another such scheme and to call once more upon your generosity, in order to defray the parish debt. In co-operating in it you would be, indeed, doing a great service to the parish, and by your charity, you would ensure a reward and blessing for yourselves.

If you are prepared to rear a stirk, please let me know as soon as possible, so that the scheme can get under way.

Be assured of my appreciation of your kindness,

I am,

Yours very sincerely,

J. L. Skelly C.C.

FIVE
Continuing efforts within the parish

The Rev. Dr. Richard Marner arrived as Parish Priest on 30 April 1876 bringing renewed enthusiasm. Already a well-travelled professor of classics and mathematics who had taken trips to Italy, Greece, Egypt, Palestine, and other countries of Europe and Asia, he continued in the role of president of Saint Malachy's, the Diocesan College, in addition to his new parish duties. The steeple, which was added to Dunsford in 1875, appears to have framed the head of Our Lady which had been discovered by Fr. Mulholland in 1791 and Dr. Marner was eager to make it part of his mission to recover the rest of the medieval statue. Rather tantalisingly it was a known fact that Aubrey de Vere Beauclerk had the base of this statue in the gardens of Ardglass Castle standing like a folly of ruination. This would have been reminiscent of sites that Dr. Marner would have seen on his travels. Unfortunately for him, the recovery of the statue did not happen until long after his departure.

The wedding of the author's grandparents Margaret Crangle and Henry Fitzsimons in April 1958, the celebrant is Canon McKee.

Today he is remembered in the parish for erecting the reredos behind the altar at Saint Nicholas'. The altar is a very significant one and if you look closely you will discover that it is more highly decorated than many others. Flanking it on either side are the two daughters of Moses, Synagoga on the left, the personification of the Jewish Synagogue, and Ecclesia on the right, the personification of the Christian Church. The imagery evoked by them was a symbol of power from the time of the Crusades. Synagoga is blind to the true church and holds on to the Tables of the Law with her left hand, and in her right she holds the spear which pierced the side of Christ on the cross. Adorning this is a flag signifying the on-going turmoil of the Crusades. Ecclesia carries forth a cross and the chalice which captured the blood that poured from the side of Christ.

Between the two statues is the crucifix. Depicted on its left, in sculptural relief, is the twelve year old Jesus sitting among the teachers in the temple, questioning them on the laws. Looking down on the scene are Joseph and Mary who had just found him after being separated during the festival of Passover. On the right hand side of the crucifix is a relief depicting Saint Peter

receiving the keys of heaven. A carving of Synagoga appears again in Massforth where Dr. Marner was subsequently appointed as Parish Priest, though this time accompanied by Christ enthroned. In Dunsford there is the monstrance, the vessel for the adoration of the Blessed Sacrament, which has been the property of the Parish of Dunsford and Ardglass since 1879.

Alterations at Saint Mary's largely retained the character of the original construction throughout the rest of the nineteenth century, although Dr. Marner did reconfigure the layout internally. The same however cannot be said of Saint Nicholas' which underwent numerous additions and, according to the account of the Rev. James O'Laverty, the church was almost entirely rebuilt by him. Both chapels though are characterised by the same steeple design. In 1901, the Rev. Fr. J.J. Donnelly established the 'Angelus Fund' to pay for bell ringers to come and ring the Angelus daily at both locations at midday and 6 o'clock.

A new parochial house, costing £550, was constructed at Chapeltown in 1913. Robbie John Magee, who was a boy of five at this time, always spoke of the carts of sand being brought up from the beach[39]. This replaced the earlier one from the 1850s, which then became an impromptu parish hall. In the 1950s it will be recalled that Margaret Gill, the Rev. Canon McKee's housekeeper, would have a stall[40] there each Sunday where she sold various religious artefacts. It also became home to a bazaar after the missions. The site for the new parochial house was given by the Gill family of Chapeltown and the field on which it stands is in Sheepland More, then known as North and South America, a name derived from its shape hugging the border with Ballyedock Upper. Two years later, in 1915, Patrick Fitzsimons, the author's great grandfather, presented the chapel with a candelabrum, most probably given in memory of his sister Ellen who had passed

---

[39] As told to the author by Alvarez Magee.
[40] The stall was sold to Lucinda Fitzsimons in the 1960s which she converted into a hen house.

away that year. At the same time a tabernacle safe and a ciborium were donated by Mrs E. Denvir and Miss Connor. The Donegal girls who worked at the harbour presented Saint Nicholas' with a candelabrum in the same year.

Ardglass was embellished with a new Lourdes Shrine in 1914, the gift of an anonymous donor which was designed by the Downpatrick architect, Thomas M. Bell, and built by P. McAleenan of Castlewellan from where the stone was quarried. Depending upon your taste you either loved it or loathed it. Under the elliptical arched canopy was an altar of Carrera marble, as well as two statues, one of Our Lady and the other of Saint Bernadette which were installed by the sculptors S. & T. Hastings. It sometimes became the centre of attention for the younger people in the village when rumours would spread that the statue of Our Lady was seen to be weeping. Vivienne Draper, daughter of the Rev. A.O. Draper, the Anglican minister, records in her memoir one such occasion. "We joined the children along the railings, eager to see the miracle. What a pretty sad face she had, I thought, and sure enough the face was wet. However just then father came driving past and, seeing us, stopped the car abruptly." Incensed by the sight of his daughter's awe at the apparent miracle he explained that it had been raining and there was probably a hole in the roof!

One of the most generous benefactors to the church at Dunsford was James Curran of Sheepland. In 1916 he passed away leaving his estate in the hands of my great grandfather Patrick and Henry Johnston who were his executors. Their role was to raise funds from the sale of the farm and provide finance for several different causes. Out of the bequest money was granted which enabled the purchase of the Stations of the Cross in 1918. James had been very keen to ensure that his spirit would rest easy and had left money for Masses to be said for him by the curate, the parish priest, and the bishop. In addition to this, he left a bequest of £1000 for the provision of a bed in the Mater Infirmorum Hospital on the Crumlin Road in Belfast. An agreement was

Estate of the late Mr. James Curran, of Sheepland, retired Farmer, deceased.

THE EXECUTORS of the Deceased desire to give Notice to the residents of the Roman Catholic Parish of Dunsford and the adjoining Parishes after-mentioned that they have entered into an Agreement with the Trustees of the Mater Infirmorum Hospital, Belfast, dated the 26th day of January, 1920, by which it is provided that in consideration of a sum of £1,000 thereby paid out of the residue bequeathed to them by the Deceased for Roman Catholic Charitable purposes, a bed in the said Hospital shall be endowed in perpetuity, together with a supply of all Medical and Surgical aid required for a Patient of the Roman Catholic Faith in the Parish of Dunsford, or the Parishes adjoining thereto, that is to say, the three Parishes of Bright, Saul and Ballee, and Kilclief and Strangford, the Patient to be nominated by Mr. PATRICK FITZSIMONS, one of the Executors of the Deceased, while living, and so long as he agrees to act in conjunction with the Parish Priest for the time being of the Parish of Dunsford, and after the death or refusal to act of the said PATRICK FITZSIMONS, of the said Parish Priest for the time being alone, a resident from the Parish of Dunsford to have the first Claim, but so long as there shall be no suitable patient from that Parish, the adjoining Parishes before-mentioned are to have for the time being the same privilege respectively in the order in which they are already named, the Patient to be a person in humble circumstances and unable to pay for hospital treatment, and to be resident at least two years in the appropriate Parish, and to be subject to the approval of the House Surgeon for the time being of the said Hospital.

Dated this 11th day of February, 1920.

H. WALLACE & CO.,
Solicitors for Executors,
Downpatrick.

raised in perpetuity with the Mater Hospital in 1920. He also left a sum of £100 for anyone in the parish who found themselves destitute, regardless of their creed. Furthermore, from his legacy donations were made to the Convent of Mercy and Saint Michael's orphanage in Downpatrick, to the Sisters of Nazareth orphanage in Ballynafeigh, and to the diocesan orphanage and the babies home in Belfast. A bursary was also established at Maynooth College for a student from the Parish of Dunsford and Ardglass or another adjoining parish.

The graveyard was further extended at Chapeltown in 1927 and was blessed by the then Bishop of Down and Connor who went on to become His Eminence Cardinal MacRory.

Disaster occurred just before Christmas on Sunday 13 December 1931, when the chapel caught fire. According to the parish record, "It was first observed a couple of hours or more after devotions. The fire started in the passage which leads from the sacristy to the Church. The alarm was raised. John Gordon, a blacksmith, who lives beside the church was first on the scene. A number of neighbours gathered and their efforts were successful in extinguishing the flames. That the church was not completely destroyed by fire was principally due to John Gordon."

When Ardglass was connected to the grid in 1937, the Sunbeam Company's acetylene plant which had been purchased for Saint Nicholas' in 1905, was moved to Dunsford. It served the building for another 18 years until the church was electrified in 1955. In Ballyhornan, a new parochial hall was gained when the deserted billets of the Northamptonshire Regiment were acquired. Secondary Masses were held here in the summer months when the population of the parish thronged with holidaymakers. This temporary accommodation was replaced by a new hall named Saint John's in 1961, and it soon became a social hub on a Friday night, where one of the regular fixtures was a band called The Polka Dots who came all the way from Omagh in County Tyrone.

Despite the Second World War and nationwide rationing, the 1940s was a period of renewed improvements, with the Rev. Fr. Maurice McHenry at the helm in Dunsford, under the direction of the Rev. Canon McKee. A new sacristy was built in 1944, as well as a new confessional. Further improvements in 1946 witnessed the creation of a new rose window depicting the aparition of the Holy Ghost at Pentecost, paid for by Bob Connolly of Sheepland and installed by the Laird family of Killough. It illuminates the sanctuary, situated as it is above the tabernacle. Judging by the windows in Saint Mary's in Chapel Lane in Belfast, it would appear that Dunsford's windows were also all replaced during this period. The earlier photograph showed a lattice design which was probably undecorated. The present windows bear the same elliptical decorative central sections. Canon McKee would have been familiar with their designs from his restoration at Chapel Lane begun in 1939, while he was administrator there. Unfortunately, when a new altar of green and white marble was erected in 1948, it meant the loss of the original wooden altar[41]. The new altar was surrounded by wooden panelling, the left side being flanked by a statue of the Sacred Heart, and the right side by one representing Our Lady. The work was quite expensive but Fr. McHenry was very pleased to announce, at the second Mass, that the construction had been paid for through the kindness and generosity of the congregation.

In the meantime, at Ardglass, Canon McKee raised sufficient funds to greatly improve Saint Nicholas' by laying a terrazzo floor, having a baptistery built and adding the Stations of the Cross. In 1947 he continued with his church improvements with the addition of two new porches, new stairs to the gallery, the solid bronze tabernacle, six bronze candlesticks and a sanctuary lamp.

---

[41] The old wooden altar would not have been consecrated, rather the divine sacrifice was performed on the altar stone. A recess may have been carved for it on the table to house it securely. The marble altar stone is preserved in the sacristy and contains two first class relics and is carved with five crosses. This altar stone, though weighty, is portable, and may date from the Penal era.

The wedding of Maureen Gill and Bob Sharp in August 1956, the celebrant is Canon McKee.

Finally, in 1949, Saint Joseph's Chapel was built on the north side of the church. When the housing estates were built on the outskirts of the town in the 1970s additional seating was added within this chapel.

So prolific a fundraiser was he that there even appeared in the newspapers of that year, an inquiry into a forty four year old will of an Ardglass man whose death was recorded in 1907 by William Clark. "On April 3rd at Ardglass, Edward Kelly, Publican, R.I.P. Offering £2.10.0 aged 80 years." Edward had left this money for Masses to be said for himself and his family or if there was another need for charitable purposes in the parish. In addition, he had shares in the Old Bushmills Distillery Company which were bequeathed, although they were of no monetary value in 1907, but which later matured to provide around £500. Canon McKee, a zealous advocate of the temperance movement, was then asked by Mr Justice Curran to prepare a case to the Attorney General. The favourable outcome of this court case can now be seen in the two fine windows, which formerly flanked the entrance to Saint Joseph's Chapel, dedicated to their benefactors Edward Kelly and his wife, Mary.

All of the aforementioned work left the parish with a large debt. Thankfully the parish had never lost touch with its largely agricultural congregation. During the 1940s Canon McKee had begun an initiative to encourage all farms to rear one animal for sale for the benefit of the parish, a custom somewhat reminiscent of the Anglo-Norman approach to raising church funds. According to stories from those who remember him, he himself would go out to the fields to inspect the animals and pick only the best.

While the importance of Dunsford had somewhat declined, it remained the burial place for the entire parish until 1956 when Canon McKee opened the new graveyard at Ardglass. He had first been inspired with the idea of the Calvary cemetery in the early 1950s and, in June 1953, permission was granted by the Most Rev.

Dr. Daniel Mageean for its planning to go ahead. The following announcement was then made on 29 August 1954. "Fr. McKee has received a quotation for the erection of a Calvary Group – (4 figures) at the entrance to the new graveyard at Ardglass. The cross will be on a pedestal 9 feet high and the cross will be 15 feet high (approx.). Figures will be six and a half feet high and in proportion. Cost will be £350." The winning tender was that of

Dr Mageean blessing The Calvary Shrine Ardglass. 4-11-1956

Tommy Rooney who built it to designs similar to those at Lourdes, Knock, and Finglas. The graveyard was paid for by a loan secured by an initial group of donors. Reimbursement of these funds was made through Calvary Masses and enrolment. The cemetery was officially blessed by Dr. Mageean on 4 November 1956.

Another aspect of parish development in which Canon McKee took a keen interest was the importance of education. He set about a plan to rebuild the two Catholic maintained schools and to establish a new intermediate school. He created the School Buildings Fund in July 1951 and raised money through weekly collections, functions, and tombolas. Within two years the funds had amounted to £6,000 and Canon McKee could, to the nearest shilling, calculate how much each street and townland in the parish had donated. Padraic Gregory's and his brother's architectural practice then drew up designs for the schemes on the most modern lines.

'No more dreaming for us. We must be very awake. 'Up and doing' is the new watchword from now onwards', blasted Canon McKee from the pulpit. The first sod was cut at 11:30 on 8 August 1952 and bricklayers commenced their work on 22 September on the Downpatrick Road. Saint Anne's Intermediate and Saint Joseph's Primary schools were blessed by Dr. Mageean on the same day in July 1954 and opened to their first intake of pupils on 6 September. The cost of Saint Anne's was £75,000. It was the first school of its kind in Northern Ireland. Unfortunately, numbers dwindled and of course it is now Saint Nicholas' Primary. Saint Joseph's, which replaced the old National School at the foot of Hill Street, cost £15,000. Six years later Saint Mary's Primary School Dunsford was replaced through further fundraising, its cost was £16,000.

The next reformation

In the early years of the 1960s the Second Vatican Council began to assemble to find a solution to the changing society which had evolved during the first half of the twentieth century. The last ecumenical council, the twentieth one, had been held nearly a century earlier and had been cut short by the Italian army which had entered Rome at the time of Italy's unification. Throughout the Catholic church there was an appetite for a new direction. In January 1965 Mass was first delivered in English in the parish. However, as the year progressed, Canon McKee's health began to decline and he was sent the Most Rev. Dr. Anthony Farquhar, then a young priest, as a Reader. Sadly, Canon McKee passed away in December of that year at the Downe Hospital. It was a few months before the new Parish Priest, the Rev. Fr. William B. Tumelty, was appointed.

Plans were then put in train for an overhaul of the decorative tastes in Saint Nicholas' for them to come into line with the new liturgy. However, before they could be enacted, Monsignor Tumelty was transferred to another parish. At Saint Mary's, in 1970, the Rev. Fr. John Fitzpatrick began alterations to the building. The gallery was taken away but, most significantly, almost all of the decoration in the sanctuary was removed. I say 'almost all' as the ceiling above the stained glass window of the Holy Ghost still retains its neo-gothic stucco grandeur. On a chance visit to the area, Fr. Maurice McHenry managed to rescue the tabernacle from the ruins of the marble altar and he brought it to Ahoghill[42] where he was then Parish Priest. The replacement altar was very evocative of the decorative taste of the time. Its construction was of an upside down wooden pyramid, veneered in Formica, and described as being reminiscent of Concorde. After the bicentenary in 1991, the chapel was renovated once again and the plans at that time returned to the original simplicity of the chapel's beginnings. The church has yet again, in the last few years, been modernised and simplified even further.

---

[42] As confirmed by a telephone call to the Rev. Fr. Hugh J. O'Hagan, Parish Priest in Ahoghill since 1994. This tabernacle matches the description of the one still in use there to this day in 2016.

The interior of Saint Nicholas' today.

Saint Nicholas' though is the church of the parish which has existed under many different guises. When the altar was being re-sited in 1982, a long forgotten addition to the chapel was discovered. The Rev. Dr. Marner had created for himself a tomb which was obviously where he had wished to be interred. Unfortunately, he had been relocated to the parish of Upper Mourne and was interred at Massforth. The most recent renovation in 2005 was carried out by Donnelly O'Neill, architects. This work, led under the direction of the Rev. Fr. Robert Fleck, completely reconfigured the floor plan and opened up the altar to the congregation, similar to the way the church's original barn plan once did. During this work the side walls, gallery, and half the length of the original aisle were removed. The trusses and altar were retained leaving the church with the dignity given to it over the years. The building has a much simpler grace about it today, with the sanctuary lit by a roof-light and modern stained glass. The church truly is a hybrid of the architecture of the Second Vatican Council and traditional ecclesiastical taste.

ST. CLEMENT, REDEMPTORIST,

PATRON
OF
RETREAT HOUSE, ARDGLASS

SIX
Mount Saint Clement

RETREAT TIME TABLE

SATURDAY

7-15 Arrival. Rooms Allotted.

7-30 Preparatory Lecture.

7-45 Tea.

8-45 Rosary in Chapel.

9- 0 Lecture. Meditation.

9-45 Night Prayers.

10-05 Retire.

SUNDAY

7-30 Rise.

7-55 Morning Prayers. Lecture.

8-30 Holy Mass.

9- 0 Breakfast.

9-30 Free time alone in Garden.

10-15 Lecture. Meditation.

11-15 Private Rosary in grounds.

11-30 Visit to the Blessed Sacrament and Examination of Conscience.

12- 0 Quiet Time for Reflection.

12-30 Lecture. Meditation.

SUNDAY—Continued

1-30 Dinner.

2- 0 Free Time alone in Garden.

3- 0 Stations of the Cross.

3-20 Confession, or Quiet time for Reflection.

4-30 Lecture. Meditation.

5-15 Afternoon Tea.

6- 0 Rosary in Chapel and Devotions for a happy death.

7- 0 Benediction and Blessings.

7-45 Supper.

8-45 Lecture.

9-30 Night Prayers.

MONDAY

Rise.	Hours
Holy Mass.	to
Holy Communion during Mass.	suit
Breakfast.	departure

SILENCE to be strictly observed during the Retreat. **SMOKING** only in Garden or Lounges.

Prayer before Retreat Talks

V. Come, O Holy Ghost, fill the hearts of Thy faithful and enkindle in them the fire of Thy love.

V. Send forth Thy Spirit and they shall be created.

R. And Thou shalt renew the face of the earth.

Let us pray.

O God Who by the light of the Holy Ghost, didst instruct the hearts of the faithful, grant that in the same Spirit we may be truly wise, and ever rejoice in His consolation, through Christ Our Lord. Amen.

Hail Mary, etc.

Sacred Heart of Jesus have mercy on us. Mother of Perpetual Succour, pray for us. All our Holy Patrons and Angel Guardians, pray for us.

Prayer to St. Clement.

Saint Clement, most faithful follower of Jesus, from your earliest years you regarded our holy Catholic Faith as your only treasure and you laboured much in making it known among the people. Obtain for us the grace that, like you, we also may value the precious gift of Faith above every other gift. Show us how to rule our actions by its holy teaching and to regard the practice of our Faith as our chief glory. Then we can joyfully repeat your words : "We confess that we are sinners and wanting in every virtue but we glory in the fact that we are children of the Holy Catholic Church."

V. Pray for us, Saint Clement,

R. That we may be made worthy of the promises of Christ.

Let us pray.

O God, Who didst adorn Saint Clement with wonderful strength of faith and with the virtue of unbroken fidelity, through his merits and example make us, we beseech Thee, so steadfast in faith and fervent in charity that we may obtain the eternal rewards. Through Christ Our Lord, Amen.

Permissu Superiorum.

73

Before the Second World War, the Belfast Co-Operative Society was running King's Castle as a hotel for their members. They had just put it up for sale as the war broke out. The government then acquired it and, when America joined the war effort, gave it to their army for use as a posting station. They then built several Nissen huts in the grounds. Thankfully, too, the army had installed running water and electricity throughout the building. However, the gardens had been left in a poor state having been torn up by tanks and there are even accounts of a dead horse having been left tied up in a tree.

Then when King's Castle in Ardglass went on the market in 1946, Canon McKee seized this opportunity to purchase another building for the parish. The opening event was a rather secular one being a 'Grand Motor Rally and Treasure Hunt' on 28 April. The debt incurred in buying such a massive building was £5,000 but it was soon cleared by a three day bazaar held in the grounds between 15 and 17 August 1946. All the items had been donated by the parishioners and arrangements were made to have everything collected and put up for auction. Among the forty items making up the prizes was a 'Rich Bride's Cake', a pair of ducks, a pair of chickens, and various items of clothing. It is important to remember all rationing only ended in 1954. The Rev. Monsignor Arthur H. Ryan of Saint Brigid's in Belfast, a friend of Canon McKee's, presided at the opening ceremony of the fair. Special buses were run from Ormeau Avenue in Belfast specifically for the event. There was a wide variety of items for the auction, including cattle, sheep, poultry, and farm produce and, in addition, entertainment was also put on and a market held.

Part of the castle was then converted into an oratory. When he was making alterations to Saint Nicholas' it was here that Canon McKee celebrated Mass. After the work had been completed, it was discovered that the Redemptorist Fathers were looking for suitable accommodation. They decided to choose Ardglass as their new base. They moved into the building in October 1946 and established their new home as Mount Saint Clement, the invocation being chosen in honour of the patron saint of their Order. The first retreat took place on 18 May 1947.

In June 1950 the grounds were home to the parish's first Corpus Christi procession. In attendance on this solemn occasion were Monsignor Arthur H. Ryan and Canon McKee's friend, the recently ordained Most Rev. Hugh Boyle, Vicar Apostolic of Port Elizabeth who bore the Blessed Sacrament. From Mount Saint Clement's the Rev. Fr. Wright, the rector, was joined by the Reverend Fathers Gorey and Deanery. Also included in the procession were the Children of Mary, the first communion children, the sodalities of the parish, and the Clonard Boys choir from Belfast. The deacon was the Rev. Fr. Neil McCamphill, curate of Down, the sub deacon, the Rev. Fr. Malachy Hurl, curate to Bright, and the Rev. Fr. Maurice McHenry, curate of this parish, was Master of Ceremonies. After leaving the grounds, the procession passed through the town finishing at Saint Nicholas'.

Dick Fitzsimons once took home a pamphlet he had been given which describes, in detail, what was required by those attending the retreat house. The retreat schedule was an intense and gruelling one but well attended by those seeking a spiritual reward. Arriving on Saturday evening attendees, who were always male, were then allotted a room. Silence was to be observed throughout the experience. Peter Davey, whose family used to rent a holiday home from Mrs. Magee opposite the gates, once told me that he often heard hushed whispers asking for the score of the latest match and Albert Colmer, whilst on his way to Sunday School, can remember being asked by men at the gates to purchase cigarettes on their behalf. The Rev. Fr. Gerard McCloskey even told me a story about an uncle of his who had once come to Mount Saint Clement for a retreat but had decided to break off early and visit a few of the town's public houses, returning to the monastery in the early hours of the morning. At breakfast he was taken aside and told that, while they couldn't fault his vocal skills, perhaps the topics he had been singing about were not exactly the correct ones for someone on a retreat.

The good relations amongst all the denominations within Ardglass continued and were such that Mount Saint Clement shared a landline with Saint Nicholas' Church of Ireland across the road. The building was run for fourteen years by the Redemptorist Fathers and then it became a convent for the Missionary Sisters of the Assumption. Its association with these two religious bodies is the reason why many people in Ardglass will still refer to the building as the monastery. After renovations were carried out, the Rev. Mother Philip Strain reopened the building as a rest home in November 1962.

Sadly, the nursing home failed and the 'for sale' signs went up once more. It was purchased by a Mr. Gilmore who wanted to convert it into a holiday resort. When this scheme didn't work out in 1974, it was then bought by Sean and Bernadette Treacy, who owned the Royal Hotel in Kilkeel. Unfortunately the restrictions of buying a listed building hindered their plans. As the building lay vacant, it fell victim to an arson attack and was saved once more from ruination by Mrs. Virginia Ward in 1982. Six years later the building was again re-opened as a nursing home and it has remained in this role ever since.

Right: Little Sisters Emiko, Helene, and Jocelyne are joined by Deirdre (second from left) of the original group.

That is the essence of our vocation, to succeed in the difficult task of making a place in our heart – as if they were the only friend we had – for all with whom we come in close contact and who the Lord places on our path.

That is the message of the Fraternity, and I want us to carry it throughout the world, over every continent, to all peoples, be they Christians, Muslims, Jews or Buddhists, Marxists, pagans or athiests.

Little Sister Magdeleine

SEVEN

The Little Sisters of Jesus

In 1994 a fraternity of three Little Sisters of Jesus made the journey to Ireland. Deirdre was returning from Canada, Phyllis who was originally from Malta was coming from Kenya, and Anne from Walsingham. Originally they were travelling through the north, with Anne as their driver, awaiting direction from the Holy Spirit as to where they should establish a new community. They spent some time living with a few different families while awaiting their call. In Ireland, the first fraternity of Little Sisters of Jesus began in Ballyfermot, in Dublin. There they lived among the marginalised travelling community. Today, throughout the world, their fraternities can be found in well over sixty countries with thirteen hundred sisters among their numbers.

The order of the Little Sisters of Jesus was established by Little Sister Magdeleine. She was a lady who, as a child from Alsace Lorraine, witnessed the conflict a land border can cause to the detriment of a society. She was also greatly afflicted throughout her life by rheumatoid arthritis and was told by a doctor to go and live in a country where there was not a drop of water. Under this instruction she went to the Sahara to live with the nomadic people. She founded the order on 8 September 1939 in Touggourt, Algeria, following the path marked out by Blessed Little Brother Charles de Foucauld.

Little Sister Anne suffered from the condition known as neurofibromatosis. The fragility of her health impacted upon the way in which the sisters could explore Northern Ireland. At that time they had located a house to rent in the former Bishop's Court R.A.F. Station at Ringawaddy. The Little Sisters of Jesus are called to live amongst those who struggle and are outcast. And so, with this as their duty, the group at Ringawaddy enjoy being in the countryside. It is here amongst those living in the houses at the former R.A.F. station that they are able to be with those personally affected by the Troubles in Northern Ireland. Usually religious Orders come to a diocese by invitation and so the unusual way in which the sisters came to reside in the area took the diocese completely by surprise. The Most Rev. Dr. Patrick Walsh, who was at the time the Bishop of Down and Connor, granted them permission to stay.

Initially their presence in the parish was kept discreet and the sisters attended Saint Mary's for daily worship. One day a member of the congregation, who had noticed their presence, asked, 'You don't mind if I ask who you are?' The response was, 'We are a group of sisters but we are living quietly here.' The phrase 'quietly here' aptly describes the approach of the Order. One of the first outreaches of the Little Sisters of Jesus was to establish a spiritual community among those living in Ballyhornan. Their outreach to the lay people among whom they live is by simply living among them, just as they do. The manner in which they achieve this is by working for their living and going out into the community. The roles in which they work are considered undesirable by much of society. The fact that the Little Sisters are there brings a presence of God, a silent prayer and a counsel of friendship, often not spoken. This simple means can evoke a strong spiritual connection among colleagues who feel that they can approach the sisters on terms of mutual respect.

Their chapel in the house where they live in Ringawaddy was found to be too cramped. The sisters were helped by many people, amongst whom were Seamus Gracey, who built them a new extension, and Sean McAlea and Brian Taggart who created a tabernacle using their woodworking skills.

Deirdre, from the original group, completed her life with the Little Sisters in 2009 and now lives among the lay people in Ballyhornan. Before her departure Little Sisters Helene and Emiko joined her in 2007. Helene, who was born in France, had spent thirty years of her religious life living among the fairground people in Switzerland. She moved around with this marginalised group each time their carnival amusements did so. She decided to stay with the group in Ringawaddy as she was strongly inspired by the work going on at the Mustard Seed Group. This group work with the disadvantaged in the area. Emiko had worked in Japan, where she was born, and also in Sri Lanka.

On 5 May 2015, the Little Sisters were shocked by the sudden death of Asia who had joined them shortly before the departure of Deirdre in 2009. Little Sister Asia, who was born in Krakow in Poland, had been confirmed by Saint John Paul II, who was then her bishop. During her time in the area, Asia had worked at Paddy's Barn where she met many people. Before her passing she established a friendship with the present Bishop of Down and Connor, the Most Rev. Dr. Noel Treanor. He visited the Little Sisters to commiserate with them at her wake. The loss of Asia to the group badly affected Little Sister Claire's health. Emotionally exhausted, she contracted encephalitis and returned to her native Belgium.

Little Sister Jocelyne joined the fraternity of sisters at Ringawaddy in January 2016. Jocelyne, who was born in France, spent years working in a factory among those affected by apartheid in a township near Capetown, and then in Johannesburg. She returned to France and was working there before coming to this parish. Prior to her calling here, she had spent many years dreaming about coming to Northern Ireland.

Whilst the Little Sisters are a predominantly Roman Catholic religious order, part of their mission is to celebrate Christianity in all its forms. In order to do this, they attend other places of worship. At the time of writing, resident with them is Sister Judith from the Anglican Order of the Sisters of the Love of God. Their form of spiritual faith is driven much in the same manner as that of Blessed Charles de Foucauld whose life was marked by the faith and hospitality of the Muslim people in the Sahara.

EIGHT
Notable parishioners

The book shown in the background of the previous page is the oldest continuous record of the parish. It was begun in 1832 by Richard Clark. He was secretary to the board of health for Ardglass during the cholera epidemic. To record his correspondence with the government he had purchased a book from the Pilson's of Downpatrick. After this period, he began to record observations of life in Ardglass, including births, deaths, and marriages. The diary also spans the era of the famine and continues until his death in December 1858. Richard lived in Kildare Street at the top of the Greenhill Steps from where he ran a shop. In addition to his he was also the owner of several boats in Ardglass. He was married to Ann, the sister of Dr. William Hamilton Smyth. Richard's daughter, Ellen, married John Fitzsimons, the author's great great grandfather.

Richard also had a son named William who was a sailor. His portrait appears in the middle of the previous page. After retiring from his seafaring days William became a spirit grocer in the Markets area of Belfast. In his later years he moved to Crossmore to live with his sister and continued to make a record of parochial events until his death in 1907. These records were written into his stock book which he brought from Belfast.

Many of the older photographs contained within this work are taken from the photographic archive held in Crossmore. Now around one hundred years in age they were taken by John MacMahon. John lived in Bath Street in Ardglass. He was an entrepreneurial man who, as well as being the town's photographer, was also a publican and farmer. The leftmost image on the previous page is a portrait of his wife Eliza and himself. Eliza was a cousin of Patrick Fitzsimons, the author's great grandfather.

The final portrait (previous page, far right) is of Henry Fitzsimons, the author's grandfather. Henry kept alive the tradition of diary keeping for parochial events just as his mother had done before him. It is thanks to his sentiment that the larger volume of resources for this work have been preserved. His love for posterity also created a collection of local history taken mainly from the *Down Recorder* newspaper. After his death in January 2009 a catalogue of all the items he kept was begun. This inventory spans an era of more than two centuries.

William Sawey

The Sawey family has had a long connection with the Lecale area and one of its most notable members was William. By trade he was a lapper – a linen inspector – for the Downpatrick linen hall. In 1792, long enough before the organisation of the United Irishmen came under scrutiny and before martial law was imposed, William was reported in the *Northern Star*, the organisation's newspaper, as chairing one of their meetings in Denvir's Hotel. Their resolution that evening was "We rejoice at the approach of that period, when irreligious intolerance shall cease, when the

The inscription on the Sawey vault at Chapeltown.

demon discord shall be banished from this land and when the Protestant and Catholic shall embrace as Christians, as brothers, as friends, and as Irishmen."

The group was made up of men who honoured their word, a fact clearly demonstrated by William Sawey. Along with two other gentlemen called Dougherty and O'Donnell, he approached William Trotter, the agent for the estate of Baron de Clifford, Lord Edward Southwell. William Trotter was a man with United Irish sympathies and so they agreed that a new Roman Catholic church should be built in Irish Street. And so it was that William's wife, Mary, née Lascelles, laid the foundation stone of the Masshouse in 1787.

It should be remembered that, although the seat of the diocese from the time of Saint Patrick had always been at Downpatrick, the town had remained for centuries after the Reformation without a church for those of the Roman Catholic faith[43]. When bishops performed ordinations, they had taken place in the ruins of ancient sites, a favourite one being at the Church of Saint Finian at Erenagh. Before the erection of the chapel on Irish Street Mass was said openly in the vicinity of Struell Wells, then beside a barn in Saul Street in Downpatrick, and latterly in a paltry cabin at Ballymote.

On his death in 1799, William bequeathed a bursary of £1000 for the education of priests at Maynooth. In 1811 his vision was realised and the Sawey Foundation was established. His wife was Catherine Johnson of Dunsford which is possibly the reason why he was interred in the cemetery at Chapeltown, rather than in Downpatrick, where he resided. The vault of the Sawey family is the oldest in that place.

---

[43] In the centre of the town, Saint Margaret's Church of Ireland was constructed on the site of an old friary. Rebuilt in 1560 as a parish church this holds the rivalled claim to be the first church built in Ireland after the Reformation.

Dr. William Hamilton Smyth

Dr. William Hamilton Smyth was born in the author's family home[44] at Crossmore on 5 July 1775. It appears that his father, Thomas, came from the distinguished Smyth family who were the landowners in Dunsford until about the turn of the nineteenth century. When Robert Hamilton Smyth, the last in the line, passed away, his only child, Mary, rightly acceded to his inheritance. In the 1659 census, the landlord of Dunsford was listed as Daniel Gowne (from the Gaeilge Uí Gabhann or Smith in English). A couple of generations previous to William's birth, in 1729, Hugh Smyth the younger had married a Mary Hamilton. Mary's father, Alexander, had been born in Killyleagh but later resided in Ballybrannagh, a townland neighbouring Dunsford. Her brother, George, had built Tyrella House with money left to him by their father. William's mother, on the other hand, was a sister of the Rev. Fr. Hugh Smyth.

In pursuit of a career as an apothecary, William trained at Lisburn but soon discovered that at this time his chosen career

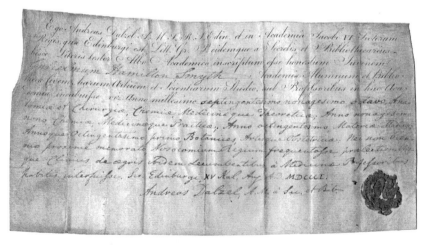

Dr. Smyth's velum parchment from Edinburgh.

---

[44] It has been discovered that Dr. Smyth is none other than the author's great great great great uncle.

was as much about diagnosing ailments as it was about providing cures and remedies. George Rice speculates that William may then have been encouraged to study medicine by his uncle Hugh. During the 1790s, the centre of the medical world was in Edinburgh. Even the funding of the journey there was quite the task. In 1798, however, William left for university possibly having secured his voyage from Donaghadee to Scotland through the generosity of his relatives in Tyrella and George has suggested to me that it is because of this that William began to use the Hamilton name.

William graduated in 1801, the year after his mother had passed away and his vellum parchment is still held in the family's archives. His dissertation, regarding the change which blood undergoes when air is taken into the lungs, (de mutationibus quas sanguis ex aere in pulmones recepto subit), is still held in the university library as confirmed by George who has consulted it. On his return to Ireland, William struck up a friendship with Ainsworth Pilson, the father of Conway and the founder of the *Down Recorder*. During his lifetime, Ainsworth compiled his 'Book of Characters'. It seems clear that this book was undoubtedly never meant to become common knowledge as it includes some rather blunt character assassinations. It is however preserved in the Public Record Office of Northern Ireland where the multitudes may consult it.

Details of Pilson's account of William reveal that "having completed his education there [in Edinburgh], he returned to his native place and in the year 1804 came to Downpatrick and stopped at lodgings. He returned to Dunsford for some time. He came back to Downpatrick where in 1811 he took a house in Saul Street where he resided until February 1833, when he removed to Irish Street in a new house then just finished by Mr. Gracey, attorney, for which he paid a fine of about £500, and subject to rent £24 yearly. Dr. Smyth is a Roman Catholic and was the first physician in this county of that religious profession. He has been gifted with a strong memory and a good natural genius, but has indulged in a way which could not be but unfavourable both to his intellect and bodily vigour. For the last thirty years since 1808 he has had good practice here, but did not accumulate money in proportion to his earnings. He never married and is remarkable for his eccentricity or the unrestrained exercise of his passions."

While the Ordnance Survey Memoirs were being recorded, it was suggested to John O'Donovan by Fr. Hugh Smyth that he should visit Dr. Smyth. A month later on Sunday 27 April 1834, O'Donovan records the hospitality he received at number one hundred and ten Irish Street, "I breakfasted with Dr. Smyth this morning: he is a very eccentric, but exceedingly learned and talented man. I introduced the subject of the snakes, but he says that there are none of them near Down, but that he is credibly informed that a gentleman has reared some near Cumber. He will ascertain the fact for me as soon as he can. He is intimately acquainted with Lecale, his practice being so very extensive, and will discover for me during the course of this day where the old Irish inhabitants of the barony reside. He shewed me his house, garden, & c. and promised to drive me out to see some places, but his time is so uncertain that I fear he will not be able to do so. I was much amused by the Doctor's learning and eccentricity."

Pilson continues: "He inherited from his father a strong constitution which by careful treatment might have endured probably to his father's age 92 but like many other men who have been blessed with such a gift he underrated its value and is now in his 63rd year but a frail vessel. He is in stature about 5ft 6ins, pretty stoutly made, light blue eyes, a large nose and quick step." On 21 January 1843, his brother-in-law, Richard Clark, recorded in his diary that "Doctor Smyth died leaving his house and books and plates to Craig and making Thos. and Henry heirs to the remainder of his property." (The reference to plates probably refers to etchings of flora and fauna.) At the age of sixty-eight William was young in comparison to his siblings and father[45]; in

---

[45] The longevity of the inhabitants in the parish was something noted in the Ordnance

fact, Dr. Smyth died only six and a half years after his father. The *Downpatrick Recorder* carried the following obituary:

Died in Downpatrick on Saturday 21st January 1843 in his 68th year, William Hamilton Smyth Esq. M.D., for many years senior physician of the town and one of the most eminent men in his profession in the North of Ireland. His name was extensively known. He possessed a most retentive memory and was distinguished for his high literary attainments. The number of respectable individuals who accompanied his remains to Dunsford, the place of his internment, manifested the respect in which he was held.

Another Dr. Smyth of Downpatrick in our time, Damian, has this to say of William in his published work *Market Street*, in stanza III of *Downpatrick:*

Dr. Smyth of Downpatrick, his
'Rare combination of great professional skill
united to high and general attainments'
with botany his peculiar study',
Is nothing to me.
              Who he is or was in 1835
is nothing compared to, 'Who *would he* be?',
the cry that calls up all his ancestry,
his townland, kin and who takes heed of him,
impressing the English of the Royal Engineers,
correcting their reconnaissance,
muttering around the Barony of Lecale,
Quoniamstown, Struell, Raholp, Ballynoe,
with Lt. Rimington of the Ordnance Survey,

Survey Memoirs. In 1834, for example, there were four parishioners in their ninetieth year, and one even older.

telling him everything.

Dr. Smyth of Downpatrick, whose
*'information can strictly be relied upon
for it is from his own personal knowledge and inquiry'.*

William Curran

The sage of Sheepland More, William, the son of William, born in 1857, went by the sobriquet of Will's Billy. He is remembered as the parish's last great seanachie[46]. Testament of his storytelling capabilities is the regard in which he is held to this very day. Will's Billy was like so many of that bygone generation, a staunch believer in the underworld of the Daoine Mhaith and a keen fiddler. He was quite often found atop Craigmalady regaling the whole countryside with his dexterous tunes. In the underworld of the men in the hill, the fiddler was regarded with great respect and music played a key role in maintaining harmonious relations between the two worlds. Will's Billy had numerous stories of visions of the ghosts and fairies which roamed the moors.

Will's Billy's home was a renowned venue for the local ceilidh. By his fireside the visitor was regaled with the most amazing tales, stories, ballads and poems. One such person would have been the surgeon Dr. Thomas Maitland Tate who thankfully had the foresight to record for posterity some of the folklore of the Sheepland coast. Dr. Tate described him as "the embodiment of the spirit that dwells within this pleasant land." Another regular visitor to his humble Sheepland home was Francis Joseph Bigger, who often came with his distinguished guests including Sir Roger Casement and Erskine Childers. Rather than rely on the written text, Will's Billy knew by heart the works of many poets including Robbie Burns, his powerful booming voice delivering each and every syllable. Padraic Gregory writes of his good friend in his *Ballad of the Blochans.*

---

[46] This title is a composite of two Gaeilge words, 'sean' and 'achaidh' meaning, quite literally, face of wisdom.

In addition to his superstitions he was also a student of nature, he dined from the catch at Sheepland harbour. Ornithology was another passion of his. He spent many days observing the many feathered songsters that are found along the rugged coastline. He passed away in 1933, at a time when modernity was beginning to ebb at the ancient customs of this part of the world.

Francis Joseph Bigger

Though a solicitor by profession, Frank, as he was known to friends, was a keen Gaeilge revivalist and contributed much to the heritage both of this parish and of the barony of Lecale, as the pages of this book will reveal. Born in 1863 at Biggerstown, near Mallusk, in County Antrim, he was a man proud of the rich Anglo-Irish culture of the island and was a staunch nationalist. His first work in the Lecale peninsula was the laying of the granite slab over the grave of Ireland's Patron Saints Patrick, Brigid, and Columba at Down Cathedral in 1899. He wanted to protect the site from constant degradation by pilgrims who regularly took away portions of the soil for souvenirs. An even worse example of this kind of unwelcome behaviour occurred in 1837, when Jonathan Binns actually took away a piece of the cross which had stood over the grave.

In 1908 he undertook the monumental task of reinstating Our Lady of Dunsford, having been able to locate all the portions of the statue. With his vested interest in Lecale's heritage at the time when the Ardglass estate went up for auction in 1911, he arrived with the intention of purchasing Ardglass Castle. Unfortunately, he was outbid by Dr. Arthur Wellington Saul McComiskey who had purchased it on behalf of Ardglass Golf Club which had already been using the grounds for fifteen years. Instead Frank decided that he should buy Jordan's and Margaret's Castles, both of which were in ruins. He set about an immediate restoration of Jordan's Castle and made it his second home.

Frank receiving his honorary Masters from Queen's University Belfast in July 1926, reproduced with permission of the Belfast Telegraph.

The castle was officially opened in October 1911 as Caisléan Séain after a ground-breaking restoration undertaken in just three short months. On the day, trains were put on especially for those who were travelling from Belfast and the town was alight with an amazing atmosphere on the occasion. The Uillean pipers were led through the town by a torch-lit procession, followed by a large gathering of locals and visitors who arrived at the tower which had the Red Hand of Ulster emblazoned on the top. Everyone was overjoyed to be in Mr Bigger's company because he had infused in them a sense of pride in the generations of the people of the Emerald Isle who had gone before.

Before the lantern slides were shown, Canon Donnelly gave an address to the assembly. 'This is the second time I have had the privilege and pleasure to welcome Mr Bigger to Ardglass – a gentleman who has shown such great pride in the land of his birth. On the last occasion we could only express our delight at having such a thorough Irishman in our midst, but today we have him again amongst us at this great gala, and we are in a position to give a real Irish Céad Míle Fáilte to the new occupier of Séan an Díomáis – a castle in which we hope to see Mr Bigger as a constant and welcome visitor, and who will always henceforth form a grand connecting link with the times when Shane O'Neill, the pride of his race and terror of his enemies, walked the streets of Ardglass.' The crowd erupted in applause.

'Mr. Bigger, generous, large-hearted, and Irish to the core as he is, does not fully understand the debt of gratitude we owe to him here in Ardglass. We hope, however, to make some recompense in a way that will be most agreeable to him – that is by making Ardglass as thoroughly Irish as he would wish to see it. We are proud of our ancient monuments as evidence of the former glory of the race, and we are glad to have Mr. Bigger amongst us, because we feel that he will infuse a new spirit of health and hope and buoyancy into us, based on our great pride in the men of our race who went before us. It is with no ordinary sense of pleasure, but with full regard to the historic character of the occasion, that I bid Mr. Bigger a hearty Céad Míle Fáilte to Ardglass; and I hope God will give him a long career of usefulness. When the history of our time comes to be written in Ulster the name of Francis Joseph Bigger will occupy an honoured position.'

Frank then rose to a standing ovation and thanked those assembled for their kind reception. He reaffirmed his point that the work he had undertaken was for an Irish identity which existed regardless of creed. After the lantern show against the wall of the castle, on the beautifully clear night, a firework display was sent up. The effect among the trees was one of a modern fairyland as they, clothed in their autumnal foliage, tinged brown against the brilliant reds and blues of the fireworks.

The revival continued and, in September 1913, the *Kerry Reporter* recorded a 'Gathering of the Gaels' at Ardglass. This occasion was the visit of William Gibson, 2nd Baron Ashbourne; Alice Stopford Green; and Sir Roger Casement to the town. A series of interesting functions were observed by the gathered crowds and these included a speech from the balcony of the parochial house by Sir Roger Casement. A torchlight procession passed through the town and a meeting was held among the Gaeilge speakers which included members of the Donegal and Scottish fishing fleets. Canon Donnelly paid tribute to Frank for the work undertaken by him for Ireland in the district. On the Sunday evening the Rev. Fr. Kelly C.Ss.R., Clonard, led the rosary in Gaeilge at the castle. Afterwards the crowd went to Mass in Saint Nicholas' where Fr. Kelly delivered a sermon in Gaeilge and unveiled two stained glass windows, the gifts of Frank.

Another function of the gathering remained untold until the 1960s when it was discussed on John Bowman's radio programme in New York. The hidden agenda was the recruitment of John McGinley and Charles Duggan who were working at the time at Ardglass harbour. Natives of Gola Island, off the Donegal coast, they were screened by Frank's illustrious guests for the purpose of manning the yacht *Asgard* sent to Germany to procure guns for the Irish Volunteers. Their landing in Ireland in July 1914 became known as the Howth Gun Running. The purpose of the weapons was originally to counteract the Larne Gun Running and to ensure the security of Home Rule which should have come into force in 1914. On the return journey they encountered the entire fleet of the Royal Navy at the outbreak of The Great War. Many of these weapons were used by the rebels during the Easter Rising in April 1916.

Later, in 1914, he undertook the restoration of two of Lecale's ancient churches at Raholp and Ardtole. In the accompanying pamphlet to commemorate the completion of the work is contained the following note:

TO
MY ESTEEMED FRIEND
THE REV. J. J. DONNELLY
PARISH PRIEST OF DUNSFORD AND ARDGLASS
GUARDIAN OF THE RESTORED SHRINE OF
OUR LADY OF DUNSFORD
PROTECTOR OF THE
HOLY WELL OF ST. PATRICK
IN THE SAME PARISH
F. J. B.

The two men did indeed form a great friendship. In Jordan's Castle Frank restored the old oratory in which, each Christmas, he set up the nativity scene. George Rice, in the first edition of *A Harvest of History*, records:

"In Mr. Bigger's Castle Ardglass at Christmas, the old chapel was renovated into a crib. Here was the manger with representatives of the Holy Child and his Blessed Mother in subdued candlelight. Fr. J.J. Donnelly with his choir came and prayers were said and a hymn sung in Gaelic followed by the Adeste Fidelis. On Saturday evening the castle was illuminated with a beacon fire and fireworks. Rockets were also sent up from the Parochial Hall, where a packed audience had assembled to hear the lecture by Mr. Bigger and see some pictures illustrating Ardglass and Lecale in history and present day aspects. Irish dancing followed. On Sunday Rev. J.J. Donnelly conducted evening devotions at the crib.

The Castle was quite inadequate to hold all who desired to attend at one session. Gaelic was used throughout."

Frank remained a prolific publisher and during his lifetime contributed to well over four hundred articles and even revived the *Ulster Journal of Archaeology*. On his death in 1926, he bequeathed Jordan's Castle to the state. It was run for a long time as a museum but unfortunately many artefacts have been lost over the years and eventually the remainder of them were taken into storage.

Richard Francis Fitzsimons

Dick, as he was known to everyone, was born on 17 February 1925. He was the fifth child of Patrick and Margaret of Crossmore. His paternal aunt was Sr. Mary St. Ninian of Nazareth House. From a young age Dick was encouraged to read and write and had instilled in him strong faithful values. In 1937 his grandmother, Margaret Anne Clinton, bequeathed to her daughter the money which she required to educate her youngest children. With his brother, Henry, already in attendance at Saint Patrick's High School in Downpatrick, Dick followed in his footsteps to the school's brand new campus on Saul Street. These two brothers were among the first generation of County Down men to receive structured higher education which was then still vocational. The school ran many extracurricular activities like drama, rugby, boxing and Gaelic sports, whilst school trips were also commonplace.

By 1941 Dick had acquired the funds to extend his studies at Saint Patrick's, having been granted a scholarship for senior studies from Down County Regional Education Committee. After completion of his studies in Downpatrick, Dick went to live in Belfast to study at Queen's University. He graduated in July 1950 with a Bachelor of Science degree, with Honours in Civil Engineering. After graduation Dick and a few friends went travelling and amongst the group was Betty McPhillips. After marrying Betty, they went to Nazareth House orphanage on the

Dick and Betty meeting with Pope John Paul II.

Ormeau Road in Belfast, where his aunt was then Mother Superior, and adopted two children, Nuala and Paul.

Like so many of his peers, he went off to South Africa where his aunt had spent many years of her mission during the Second Boer War at the turn of the twentieth century. Shortly after emigrating, Dick joined the prestigious civil engineering firm of White and Bowyer while, at the same time, also studying Quantity Surveying at the University of Natal. With this practice Dick was constantly on the move to such places as Bulawayo and Lusaka before settling permanently in Blantyre in Nyasaland in 1957 and becoming partner in the business.

In 1958 Dr. Hastings Kamuzu Banda, 'the Black Messiah', leader of the Nyasaland African Congress, denounced the British federation. Violent clashes between Congress supporters and colonial authorities on 2 March 1959 led to his imprisonment. After his incarceration, the African National Congress conducted a 'big swoop'. A state of emergency was declared. After his release, Banda attended talks with the British government on constitutional reform. Prime Minister, Harold MacMillan, was greeted by nationalist demonstrations as the country was, as Dick phrased it, "growing tired of the way Britain [was] handling the affairs of Africa."

During the state of emergency Dick wrote a letter to his brother, Henry, describing, in graphic detail, the severity of the situation.

Another member of this parish, Tim Magennis, a good friend of Dick's, became embroiled in a high profile libel case, in March 1963, while working for the *Rhodesia Herald* and writing a piece entitled 'Dr. Banda Rides Round in Pomp'. As Europeans, the two men of this parish were living in a precarious position. Banda had been appointed Prime Minister of the self-governing Nyasaland and had declared independence, as Malawi, in 1964. He went on to appoint himself president for life in 1971, leading to a one party state and the suppression of opposition movements. It was to be fourteen years before the first elections were held with all candidates having to be approved by Banda after he submitted them to an 'English test.'

A diplomatic and true gentleman who was described by his business partner Paul Harris as 'upright, kind, patient, generous and loving', Dick was appointed by the Irish government to the role of Honorary Irish Consul in 1965, one year after the founding of Malawi, retaining this role until his death on 4 April 1991. On his 41st pastoral pilgrimage, Saint John Paul II arrived in Malawi. In his address to the people he declared, "As a true friend of Malawi, I wish to encourage you all – the President, Government and people of this beautiful country – to persevere with courage and dedication in building a society worthy of the highest ideals." During this visit Dick had the privilege of meeting the Pope.

Having founded his own practice in 1962, Dick dedicated his guiding hand to the training of surveyors in developing countries. He became a moderator of surveying examinations for the University of Malawi as well as holding membership of the Royal Institute of Chartered Surveyors, the Chartered Institute of Arbitrators and the Surveyors Institute of Malawi, to mention just a few.

A member and former chair of the Rotary Club of Blantyre from 1958, Dick lived up to the Rotarian approach to advance the world with understanding, goodwill, and peace through the improvement of health, the support of education, and the alleviation of poverty which resulted in his being awarded the Paul Harris Fellow Award, the highest award bestowed in honour of the founder of this worldwide organisation. At Dick's untimely death in 1991, condolences to Betty, Paul, and Nuala came from a variety of people and numerous establishments from the world of industry and infrastructure. Following his death, the Blantyre Rotarians set up the Dick Fitzsimons Memorial Rotary Trust Account and donations to this were faithfully administered to deserving causes, so that their friend and colleague will continue to be remembered in times to come.

and fitty three.

To the honour
and glory of God,
and under the
patronage of the
ber Blessed Virgin.

✠

They who instruct
many

into righteousness
shall shine as stars
for all eternity."

Daniel XII C. 3 V.

NINE

Vocations from the parish

Throughout the last few centuries there have been numerous people from the parish who have been called to Holy Orders. Over time their stories have crossed over and have been woven into the greater fabric of the Diocese of Down and Connor. On 10 December 1976, the Rev. Fr. Charlie Cross was ordained at Saint Mary's, the church's first ordination in its history. We now take a look back at those individuals from the parish who have added to the religious tapestry of the diocese.

Patrick O'Prey

Born in the parish of Dunsford in 1647 Patrick was ordained by Saint Oliver Plunkett in 1671. In 1704 he proceeded to Downpatrick to register as Parish Priest of Ballyphilip. He is thus the first member of this parish recorded as minister there beginning this parish's long association with that part of the diocese. During the Glorious Revolution he appears to have taken a prominent role in the Jacobite army. He is returned as "Patrick O'Prey, Clerk, of the Little Ardes" in the list of adherents of James II who were convicted of high treason at Banbridge on 10 July 1691. He died in the year 1717 and was interred in the medieval parish graveyard at Saint Mary's Church of Ireland at Dunsford, though no memorial marks his grave.

Eugene Megarry

A native of Crossmore, the Rev. Fr. Eugene was Parish Priest of Saul and died in 1763 or 1764. He was buried in the medieval parish graveyard. As Parish Priest at Saul, there being no chapel, Mass was said amongst the ruins of the old abbey built in the twelfth century by Saint Malachy, Bishop of Down. The mortuary house on the site there was repaired and became a confessional – hence its second name of Saint Patrick's Confessional.

William Megarry

Brother of Fr. Eugene, William graduated from the University of

Sorbonne in Paris, having achieved a doctorate. He was appointed Parish Priest of Dunsford and Ardglass and later became the Dean of Down. The Rev. Dr. William Megarry was responsible for removing the body of the statue of Our Lady of Dunsford to his residence at Crossmore, Megarry's Hill, a ridge overlooking the old parish church. After his death in 1763, he was interred at the medieval parish graveyard alongside his brother.

Daniel Megarry

Born in 1702 at Crossmore, Daniel was a nephew of the Rev. Dr. William Megarry, Parish Priest of Dunsford and Ardglass and of the Rev. Fr. Eugene. Daniel was commonly known as Donal Mór and was curate at Saul in 1725. From here he was appointed Parish Priest of the Ards in 1732. Later he was appointed as Parish Priest to Kilmegan in 1752. After his death on 15 January 1784, he was interred with his uncles at Dunsford. The memorial slab, which is laid flat over the length of the grave has for some time been broken into three pieces.[47]

Daniel Clinton

Born in Sheepland, the Rev. Fr. Daniel was Parish Priest of Dunsford and Ardglass while also the administrator for Kilclief. Whilst in Kilclief, Fr. Clinton assembled people among the rocks in Ballynarry at a place called Paracanary and celebrated the stations in an adjacent field. The stone on which he celebrated Mass was removed to the old chapel at Kilclief where it can be seen to this day. He was buried in the medieval parish graveyard after his death on 8 October 1788[48], aged seventy-seven. His memorial tablet built against the boundary wall reads:

IHS
Here lie the re-
mains of the Revd.
Daniel Clinton Pastor
of Dunsford who
depd. this life 8 Octr.
1788 Aged 77 years. Lord
have mercy on
him.

---

[47] This stone erected in memory of ye, Revd. Daniel Magarry pastor of, kilmegan who departed yis life 15, Iany. 1784 aged 82 years & also in, Memory of his two uncls ye. Revd., Eugine & ye. Revd. wm. Magarry pastors of, saul & Dunsford wm. being Dean of Down Bachelor of arts & doctor of, Sorbon

[48] In Sheepland is an old farm named Knockdoo. There is a local story that, until the middle of the last century, a light used to shine from the ruins of the cottage towards Chapeltown during the October devotions. The tradition associated with this phenomenon was that there had been a priest, possibly by the name of Fr. Clinton, whom someone in the parish disliked. They tied the doors of the house shut and sealed the chimney, thereby inducing death by smoke inhalation. The light only ceased its annual appearance after Mass was offered for the tormented soul of the cleric.

Daniel O'Doran

Born in Ardtole[49], the Rev. Fr. O'Doran officiated in his home parish as curate and then Parish Priest from 1758 to 1766. In 1768 he was appointed Parish Priest of Ards, and was the last priest to hold the entire peninsula as a single parish. Twelve years later he succeeded to the appointment of Parish Priest of Kilcoo where he died five years later after a fall from his horse whilst on a sick call. He was interred in the ancient church of Ballytrustan near Portaferry and over his grave are inscribed the words:

> Here lieth the body of Rev. Daniel O'Doran, heretofore Parish Priest of the Ards. He departed this life 17th June, 1785, aged 50 years. He was a man of benevolent disposition, a stranger to bigotry, a facetious companion, and universally lamented by a numerous acquaintance.

John Fitzsimons

A native of Ross, the Rev. Fr. John Fitzsimons served as curate to the Rev. Fr. Daniel O'Doran in the Parish of Ards until it was divided up in 1780 after the departure of Fr. O'Doran and the Parish of Ballyphilip (Portaferry) was created and he was appointed the first Parish Priest there[50]. After serving there for five years he was

---

[49] According to the account of the Rev. Monsignor James O'Laverty, the Rev. Fr. Daniel O'Doran was from County Armagh. The record describing him as a native of Dunsford and Ardglass comes from the account of priests in the Bicentenary Book for Ballyphilip parish.

[50] Angus Na Naor Ruaidh O'Daly, a bard of the old Irish court who suddenly found himself out of work after the Flight of the Earls, was encouraged by Sir George Carew and Lord Deputy Mountjoy to satirise the remaining Irish landlords on their estates. His account of the Savages of the Ards was recorded by John O'Donovan in the Ordnance Survey letters to Lieutenant Larcom at Phoenix Park.

> In the Ards of Uladh, scarce and starving,
> A country without happiness without religion,
> Where Savage the foreign hangman,
> Scrapes off the limpets with his knife.

Further expanding on this O'Donovan interjects:

> Next in my course I came to the Ards, High Ground

appointed to Kilcoo in 1785, just after the death of Fr. O'Doran. Fr. Fitzsimons "was present and encouraged the defenders at the Battle of Ballynagapog, on the road from Ballymoney to Rathfriland, for which he was censured by the clergy both of his own diocese and the Diocese of Dromore. He died about the year 1798."[51]

Thomas Clinton

The Rev. Fr. Thomas Clinton was the nephew of the Rev. Fr. Daniel although, unlike him, he never attended college and was thus never appointed to any parish. On his death, which Richard Clark recorded on the 7 August 1847, he was buried in the chapel yard at Dunsford. Though there is no marker to remember him by, a few anecdotes of Fr. Thomas Clinton are recorded by the Rev. Dr. George Crolly in the *Life of the Most Rev. Doctor Crolly*:

Amongst the special favourites of the Primate, whilst he remained in Down and Connor, was Father Clinton – a genuine specimen of the kind-hearted, pious, devoted, and somewhat eccentric priest of the old school.

Once, whilst Mr. Clinton resided in Downpatrick, he went, as usual, to the chapel to say Mass in the

Where I nor pleasure nor religion found
Here dearth and hunger hold their ghastly reign
And all are Savage, brutal and profane
The Savage chief is savage too by name
A foreign rascal never known to fame
By feats of arms, or loftiness of soul!!
This dastard hath nor bread nor herds nor flocks
But lives by scraping limpets off the rocks!!
Before the creation of the parish of Ballyphilip there had only been one Parish Priest assisted by one curate for the whole peninsula. This is in spite of the fact that the Savages remaining Catholic until 1812. The area is home to one of the oldest Presbyterian congregations in Ireland. The Presbyterian congregation at Portaferry refused to conform to the will of Charles II during the Restoration and have been worshipping since 1665.
[51] Page 43, *An Historical Account of the Diocese of Down and Connor*, Vol. I.

morning. After he had vested in the sacristy, and gone up to the platform of the altar, he was observed to search his pockets very carefully. At length he turned round to the people, and said solemnly, commencing by a soliloquy – 'Well, Job, you had your trials, no doubt, but, on my word, other persons have their trials too.' Then, addressing the congregation, he continued – 'My good people, I forgot my spectacles and unless some of you will go down the street for them, I cannot say Mass.'

He was not only a sober, but a most abstemious man, and seldom tasted spirits, or even wine. He once consented to take a glass of punch after dinner, at a respectable farmer's house, where he dined. The moment he had swallowed a small quantity of it, he started up and roared out, 'Son of Moses, you have poisoned me.' This sudden and vehement declaration created the greatest confusion in the assembled company, the prevailing impression being that he had gone mad. It was ultimately discovered, however, that there had been turpentine in the glass which he had used and, when the matter was thus satisfactorily explained, he enjoyed the laugh which his abrupt and extraordinary exclamation occasioned as much as any of the company.

Such was the relationship between the Most Rev. Dr. William Crolly and himself that Fr. Clinton would, without any qualms about so doing, verbally rebuke the opinion of the bishop if he believed him to be wrong.

William Crangle

The Rev. Fr. William Crangle was born in Sheepland and, after ordination in 1778, he went to the College of Saint Vadastus in Douai where he gained a Bachelorship of Philosophy. The following memorandum is entered in a volume of MS sermons in Fr. Crangle's handwriting: "July the 8th, 1783, William Crangle bid the last farewell to Doway, in nomine domini, Amen. November 20th, 1783, I commenced in Belfast, and departed from it on May's eve, 1787, and commenced to Dunsford, where I remained until 25th of said month; and on 26th May, 1787, I celebrated Mass in Glenavy."[52]

Whilst Parish Priest of Glenavy, he lived with his brother at a place called Darachrean which was still known at the end of the nineteenth century as Crangle's Hill. The Masshouse built in 1760 was destroyed by seven or eight local people known as 'The Wreckers' in 1796. Fr. Crangle continued to celebrate Mass within its ruins until 1802 when he received compensation and rebuilt it and this modest thatched roof building was replaced in the 1860s. After his death, the Rev. Fr. Crangle was interred outside his chapel with his grave today being located near the sacristy door.

Hugh Smyth
Born at Crossmore in 1759, the Rev. Fr. Hugh Smyth was ordained at Erenagh in the ruins of the Church of Saint Finian by the Most Rev. Dr. MacMullan. Afterwards he proceeded to the Irish College in Paris where, shortly after his arrival there, the French Revolution broke out. As a cleric he was seen as a member of the establishment which necessitated the need to disguise himself as a doctor in a hospital in order to escape the guillotine and, in so doing, he acquired medical knowledge. On his return to Ireland he was soon being visited by people seeking cures as well as penance. He was appointed administrator to the Rev. Fr. John Fitzsimons at Kilcoo[53] in 1794 and, on whose death, succeeded him as Parish Priest.

---

[52] Page 329, *An Historical Account of the Diocese of Down and Connor*, Volume II.
[53] Kilcoo is the location of the church where the people of Armagh believed they mourned the body of Saint Patrick. It comes from the Gaeilge Cill an Chumhadh. A row had broken out at the Quoile estuary between these people and the people of Down and, to break it up, a wall of water came up in the estuary to separate the people. Two oxen appeared

After his appointment he built himself a chapel, though this has since been replaced. Whilst at Kilcoo he got into difficulties and was assaulted by Thomas Fitzpatrick, Edward Rush, James Boden, and Daniel McCartan who prevented him from celebrating Mass on 11 April 1813. With these problems continuing, he resigned from Kilcoo in 1814 and was subsequently moved to Newtownards, continuing as Parish Priest. He left there in 1817 when he was appointed to the parish of Blaris (Lisburn) where he was visited at the time of the recording of the Ordnance Survey Memoirs by John O'Donovan, who wrote this of his encounter with the Rev. Fr. Hugh:

I called this evening on the Revd. Mr Smyth. Roman Catholic Priest of the district of Lisburn which comprises eight Protestant parishes around the town of Lisburn. He is a very old man who was educated in France and I was struck with the amazing difference between the ease and refinement of his manners and the hauteur of petty country landlords. When I told him what I was about, he said, 'Sir, I shall be very happy to lend all the assistance in my power to promote your object but in this part of Ireland it is very often difficult to ascertain the correct names of places, I am afraid you are 100 years too late.' He shewed me into his little parlour, and then commenced to tell me about the kindness of the Marquis of Downshire towards him in giving him one acre and a half free of rent to erect a chapel and burial place, and some money to assist in its erection. He never asked what religion I was of, he wished I would call tomorrow to see his chapple. His venerable appearance and square velvet cap reminded

---

with the corpse and proceeded with the Armagh people. This, however, was a mirage which disappeared just before they reached Armagh, by which time the people of Down had buried Saint Patrick on the Cathedral hill.

me of the old patron saints of Irish churches. He is of the opinion that the round towers were of some ecclesiastical purpose, but what the particular purpose was, he thinks can never be satisfactorily explained. I told him that I had heard that snakes were now abundant in the neighbourhood of Downpatrick and that I was exceedingly anxious to ascertain the truth of that report, but, Sir, says he, 'If you have any curiosity to ascertain its truth or falsehood call upon my nephew Dr. Smyth of Downpatrick, who is well acquainted with the zoology of the whole county, and he will give you every information on that head. As for me I would not believe any report on that subject until I saw it corroborated by fact and attested by men of veracity'. I told him that some people shewed an unwillingness to give me information. He said that some people are afraid of any one going about lest he might be a spy, and the subject of tythes is so much agitated that people are afraid of anyone sent from the government but he says, 'All this is from pure ignorance. Give my compliments to any of the persons I have mentioned to you and you will find that they will render you any service they are able and anything I can do for you it will afford me a satisfaction to do it.' I have written this letter to commemorate my conversation with this old man, one of a class of men who will soon be extinct in Ireland, i.e. old priests educated on the continent. He is very feable in body but rather vigorous in mind, considering his great age.

He spent his latter years in Lisburn and died on 18 November 1839 and was interred in the nave of the chapel at Lisburn. John O'Donovan was correct in assuming that the Rev. Fr. Hugh Smyth was of a dying breed as Maynooth was established in 1795 providing the authorities of the Crown with a means of monitoring the activities of the Irish clergy and keeping them apart from the influence of the French revolutionaries.

John Magee

A native of Corbally, after ordination in Downpatrick by the Most Rev. Dr. MacMullan, the Rev. Fr. John Magee was appointed to the parish of Blaris, then an arduous mission, as at that time there had been a military camp founded there in response to the perceived threat from the United Irishmen. He and Fr. Peter Cassidy had, on 16 May, 1797, accompanied four privates of the Monaghan Militia who had been condemned to death by court martial from Belfast to the place of execution at Blaris camp. *The Northern Star* reported:

> Daniel Gillan, Owen McKenna, William McKenna, and Peter McKenna, privates in the Monaghan Militia, who had been tried by a court martial in Belfast, were conveyed to Blaris Camp on cars, accompanied by two priests (Rev. John Magee and Rev. Peter Cassidy, C.C., Belfast) and by a strong guard of horse and foot, and shot at two o'clock. They seemed very sensible of the awful change they were about to make; and at the time behaved with the greatest firmness, choosing to die rather than turn informers.

Later Fr. Magee worked at Ballee as Parish Priest. He was undoubtedly a distinguished man as he always wore a three cocked hat. His predecessor, another Fr. Magee, and he were always told apart by the nickname 'three cocked-hat'. When he died in 1808 he was interred in Kilclief churchyard.

Edward McQuoid

A native of Ballybrannagh in the parish of Dunsford[54], the Rev. Fr. Edward McQuoid was ordained in August 1800 by the Most Rev. Dr. Patrick MacMullan, Bishop of Down and Connor, and officiated in Derriaghy, assisting the Rev. Fr. Hugh O'Donnell, Parish Priest of Belfast. He was appointed Parish Priest of Ballyphilip in about 1812. He died suddenly in October 1815, aged about thirty-nine, and was interred in Dunsford.

Robert Denvir

A native of Ballybeg, records of his priesthood are elusive. Richard Clark records that a "Priest Denvir left this parish for Saul" in March 1843. He appears to have risen to the rank of Parish Priest though his monument in Dunsford does not record his parish. He died on 17 September 1877 at the age of sixty-four.

James Killen

A native of Tollumgrange, the Rev. Fr. James Killen entered the Logic Class at Maynooth on 4 September 1828 and was ordained by the Most Rev. Dr. Murray in 1832. He served as a curate in Randalstown and as an administrator in Ahoghill, and then he assisted the Rev. Fr. Hugh Smyth in the same post at Lisburn. From here Fr. Killen was appointed Parish Priest to Ballee in 1837. While there, he negotiated the extension of the ground and had the graveyard consecrated.

Subsequently he was appointed Parish Priest to Ballyphilip in March 1843, where he remained until his death. Almost immediately he began improvements to Saint Patrick's chapel, which is located outside Portaferry, in Tullyboard townland. He was the person responsible for reordering the building into its

---

[54] Technically in the Parish of Ballee, this attribution may stem from a time when the Rev. Fr. William McAlea was Parish Priest of the parishes of Ballee, Dunsford and Ardglass, and Kilclief. In Ballybrannagh there was also a Mass station immediately adjacent to the townland of Tollumgrange.

present form, having enlarged the church with a new extension creating the T- shaped plan and also erecting the galleries. Later, after acquiring an acre of land from Colonel Andrew Nugent in 1853, he erected the parochial schools[55] which were dedicated under the patronage of the Blessed Virgin, and extended the graveyard. In addition to this he acquired three and a half acres and built the parochial house.

In 1879 he continued to embellish Portaferry by erecting two further altars – on the Gospel side one honouring Saint Patrick and on the Epistle side one honouring the Blessed Virgin, the cost of £500 being paid for by the Murphy sisters of Tara. In addition to this, the gift of the chalice to Fr. Killen in 1848 is still used there. He died on 6 February 1881, aged seventy-five, whilst celebrating his jubilee year, having served Ballyphilip for thirty-eight years. Many years later, in the latter half of the twentieth century, the Killen family of Tollumgrange had Fr. James' altar stone returned to them by the Crangle family of Portaferry.

Hugh Hanna
A native of Crossmore, the Rev. Fr. Hugh Hanna's obituary from 13 June 1885 reads:

---

[55] The inscription on the National School built at Portaferry has been selected as this chapter's image.

DEATH OF REV. HANNA, PP BRYANSFORD

Again the shadow of death has fallen on the priesthood of Down and Connor. It was our duty last week to announce the death of a zealous and pious young priest, Father Magorrian, whose corpse weeping thousands followed on Thursday last from St. Malachy's to his long home in Milltown. It was then a young oak that had suddenly been riven by the lightening flash. To-day an old oak, hoary with age and venerable among the giants of the forest has been prostrated – the Rev. Hugh Hanna, the Parish Priest of Bryansford, the parish in which the late father Magorrian had been born and reared, breathed his last on last Saturday morning at 7 o'clock. Father Hanna was born in Crossmore, in the Parish of Dunsford, Co. Down in August 1812. He studied the classics in Downpatrick at the celebrated school of Dr. Nelson.

He entered the logic class of Maynooth College on 26th August, 1833, and was ordained in Belfast by the Most Rev. Dr. Denvir, on the 10th August, 1836. At first he was appointed curate in Belfast, immediately after his ordination, where he laboured zealously until his appointment as administrator of Rasharkin, County Antrim, on 20th March, 1839. There he remained until he was appointed Parish Priest of Maghera or Bryansford, County Down, on the 14th February 1845. Father Hanna had attained to a very venerable age, and had almost reached the year of his golden jubilee of the priesthood. Every one of his many years was filled with honour and dignity. Seldom or ever did a reaper go forth in the vineyard of the Lord to gather such a rich harvest of souls. To him we may well apply the words of Our Lord, "I have chosen you and appointed you that you should go forth and bring forth fruit and your fruits should remain." These words are particularly applicable to the late Father Hanna. His labours were unceasing. He was honoured and respected as a pious and holy man, not only by his own parishioners but by everyone who knew him.

Whilst at Dunloy, he greatly assisted in the erection of Saint Joseph's which was dedicated in September 1840. Later in 1845, almost immediately on his appointment to Maghera, he constructed old Saint Mary's at Newcastle. This chapel was blessed by the Most Rev. Dr. Denvir with £225 collected on the day, during which Dr. Denvir also held a confirmation.

Richard Killen

Brother of the Rev. Fr. James Killen, but unlike him, Fr. Richard entered the Rhetoric Class at Maynooth. This was on the same day that Hugh Hanna entered the Logic Class, both men having already been known to each another. Richard was ordained by the Most Rev. Dr. Healy, Bishop of Kildare, on 3 February 1839. He assisted his brother, James, as curate in Ballee before becoming administrator in Ballykinlar in 1842. Subsequently he was appointed to Lisburn as administrator in 1847 and was appointed Parish Priest of Coleraine one year later and it was whilst he was there that he erected the chancel.

Returning to Lecale in 1856 as Parish Priest of Bright, he is responsible for the erection of Saint Patrick's, Legamaddy, which celebrated its one hundred and fiftieth anniversary in 2015. On the death of his brother, he was appointed his successor in Ballyphilip. William Clark records under deaths: "1898 November 28th Father Richard Killen at Portaferry aged 84 years offering £24.0.0. P.P." Both brothers were interred at Portaferry under the obelisk erected by Fr. Richard in 1881.

George Conway

Native of the parish, Fr. Conway entered the Diocesan Seminary in August 1845 and proceeded to the Irish College in Paris in 1847. He returned and was ordained by the Most Rev. Dr. Whelan, Bishop of Bombay, in Dublin in October 1852. He served in Belfast before being appointed to Derriaghy where he rebuilt Rock Church. Fr. Conway also served in Carnlough for a few months in 1889 and then in Glenavy from 1890 until his retirement in 1894.

Patrick McConvey

The Rev. Fr. McConvey of Tollumgrange entered the seminary in 1844 and subsequently, in 1848, the Logic Class at Maynooth. He was ordained 18 September 1852 by the Most Rev. Dr. Whelan, Bishop of Bombay, with Richard Clark recording, "Revd. Patrick McConvey celebrated Mass for the first time in Dunsford Chapel on Sunday 17th October 1852 after being ordained in Maynooth." He officiated at his first funeral shortly afterwards when Mrs. Megraw, wife of James the shoemaker in Ardglass, passed away on 25 October.

He was soon afterwards appointed as a curate in Downpatrick and later moved to Belfast. He became Parish Priest at Newtownards in 1864 and his name is recorded in a Latin inscription on the foundation stone at Comber which was laid by the Most Rev. Dr. Dorrian. Prior to the completion of the chapel in 1871, he celebrated Mass above the Market House and in a building in The Crescent. Fr. McConvey secured the ground forever from Elizabeth, the Dowager 4th Marchioness of Londonderry, who was a convert to Catholicism. He also erected a further two churches – the church at Newtownards at the sole expense of the Dowager which was dedicated in 1877, and the new church at Bangor which was dedicated in 1887. He died in 1890 and was interred on the south side of his new church at Newtownards.

Patrick Clarke

"11th February 1851 Patt Clark went to R.C. Seminary Belfast and to Maynooth 26th August 1853" records Richard Clark. Born in Ardtole, he entered the Humanity Class at Maynooth and was ordained in 1858. He officiated as curate at Newtownards, Ballymacarrett, and Saint Malachy's and later was made the first administrator at Saint Mary's, Chapel Lane, in 1866. At that time the first church, which had been built in 1784 through the generous assistance of the Presbyterians of the town, was crammed to the rafters each Sunday. Additional services did not remedy this problem and so the architect, John O'Neill, was appointed to extend the church in the Romanesque style.

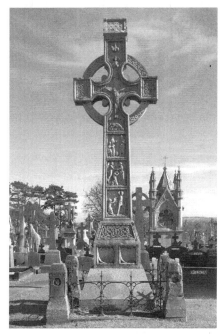

Fr. Clarke's memorial cross at Milltown cemetery.

Fr. Clarke died in Belfast on 15 November 1869 and was interred at Milltown Cemetery, this being the first burial in that place and the first priest to die on the mission in Belfast, with the sole exception of the Most Rev. Dr. Denvir. His grave, which he shares with the Rev. Fr. James Canavan, is to be found at the entrance to the graveyard under the tallest high cross in that place.

James Kennedy

Born at Ardglass in 1852, he studied at the Diocesan College and went on to the Natural Philosophy Class at Maynooth in 1872. The Rev. Fr. James Kennedy was ordained by the Most Rev. Dr. Dorrian in Saint Malachy's in 1876 and was appointed as curate to

Randalstown, followed two years later to Ballymena, to Duneane in 1882 and to Saint Malachy's in 1883. He was appointed Parish Priest of Glenravel in 1890, remaining there for nineteen years.

From 1909 to 1916 he acted as Parish Priest at Antrim where he was served by the Rev. Fr. Patrick McNamara as curate. He became a Canon after he was appointed to Ballyphilip in 1916. One of the first things he did there was to purchase a house in Shore Street for his curate and, in the following year 1917, he purchased a field for a new cemetery. At Ballyphilip he added the reredos behind the altar in September 1923, meaning that the present appearance of Saint Patrick's interior has been created through the efforts of two priests native to the parish of Dunsford and Ardglass. Canon Kennedy died one year after his retirement in 1928 and was interred at Portaferry.

Patrick O'Connor
Born in Tullomgrange on 25 April 1861, the Rev. Fr. Patrick O'Connor studied at Saint Malachy's and entered the Logic Class at Maynooth on 3 September 1880. He was ordained there by the Most Rev. Dr. Logue, later to become a cardinal, on 7 July 1885, and was appointed to his first curacy at Ballykinlar on 1 August of that year. His career ended abruptly on 16 April 1904 with William Clark recording his death "at Ballydock Revd. Patrick Connor aged 42 years R.I.P. suddenly of heart disease." After his death he was interred in the grave of the Rev. Fr. Peter Denvir at the chapel yard at Dunsford. His name completes the inscriptions on the memorial slab there:

In memoriam etiam Revd. Patrith O'Connor vicarii qui natus est apud Tullumgrange Aprilis viginto Quinto MDCCCLXI, ordinatus est Julii VII MDCCCLXXXVI mortuus est Aprilis XVI MDCCCCIV

James O'Flaherty

Born in Ardglass in July 1865, James entered Saint Malachy's College in January 1877. He proceeded to the Logic Class at Maynooth in September 1885. He graduated with a Bachelor of Arts in October 1885. Fr. O'Flaherty was ordained in the Diocesan College by the Most Rev. Dr. Patrick McAllister four years later in July 1889. His first appointment was to the curacy of Saintfield in that same year. The following year he was appointed to Castlewellan, then to Glenravel in 1892, and to Cushendall in 1895. In 1901 he was to be found living as a boarder in the role of curate in Holywood. In 1909 Rev. Fr. O'Flaherty was appointed Parish Priest at Armoy, where he remained until 1935. During his time there, in 1923, he substantially altered Saint Olcan's church.

Margaret Fitzsimons

Born in Crossmore in September 1865, Margaret was called, in 1891, to join the Sisters of Nazareth in Hammersmith. She was given the religious name of Sister Mary St. Ninian. Her father's uncle was the primate, the Most Rev. Dr. William Crolly. She was sent with a group of her peers in 1895 to found a convent for the order in Durban, South Africa, where she became bursar. Three years later, in 1899, she was moved to Kimberley where she was during the one hundred and four day siege during the Second Boer War. The sisters opened their convent as a convalescent hospital treating soldiers impartially. It was of course one of the last gentlemen's wars and no shells were fired on Sundays. Later she became Mother Superior in Johannesburg.

Sister St. Ninian was located at Ballynafeigh in Belfast during the troubles of the 1920s, working as Mother Superior. Leaving there she was then sent as Mother Superior to found a Nazareth House in San Diego in 1924 at the invitation of the Most Rev. John J. Cantwell, Bishop of Los Angeles. In 1929 she was appointed Mother Superior of the convent she had helped to found in Durban. Her next appointment was as Mother Superior at Port

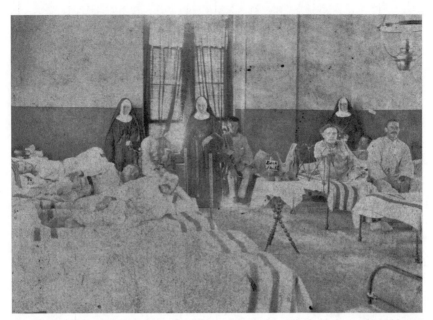

Sr. Ninian (in centre) in the convalescent hospital in Kimberley, on the table are shells which fell into the convent.

Elizabeth in 1934 where she celebrated her jubilee in 1941. Sister St. Ninian returned to Ballynafeigh in 1946 as Mother Superior of Nazareth Lodge Children's Home. Whilst here she found time to visit her native parish. She retired in 1950 and died in 1954 at the age of eighty-nine having given sixty-four years of service. In her Christmas 1947 letter she wrote, "I had the great pleasure of visiting Dunsford Chapel much improved but still the same to me. I used to sing in the Choir, and one Sunday Rev. Dr. Marner, told me I sang too loud."

James McGrath

Born at Ardglass in 1877, the Rev. Fr. James was the only son of William and Ellen McGrath. He entered Saint Malachy's in September 1892 and, after completing a secondary course, went to the Irish College in Paris. His ordination was performed by the Most Rev. Dr. Walsh in June 1902. His first curacy was in Kilcoo, followed by Holywood where he served under the Rev. Monsignor James O'Laverty, diocesan historian. After working in Blaris for five and a half years, he moved to Lower Mourne in 1909, followed by three years in Dunloy until 1912, and then for a time in Duneane.

After this he returned to Belfast and was appointed curate to Saint Joseph's Belfast, before continuing to work at Saint Peter's Cathedral. He died in July 1941 at Kilcoo, the parish he had returned to preside over as Parish Priest twelve years previously. Whilst there he won the affection of his parishioners by making several improvements which included the renovation of the schools in the parish.

Patrick O'Kelly

Born at Ardglass in 1878, the Rev. Fr. Patrick O'Kelly studied at the Diocesan College and entered Maynooth in 1899. He was ordained on 18 January 1903 and celebrated his first Mass the following day. Fr. O'Kelly's first appointment was as curate to Loughgiel. Following this he was transferred to the parish of Upper Mourne as curate. After this period, he continued in the role of curate at Saint Brigid's in south Belfast and in 1916 was

Fr. Patrick O'Kelly. Photograph courtesy of Tomás Mac Thréinfhir.

transferred to Saint Patrick's in Donegall Street. He remained here throughout the troubles of 1922 and the following year, when the Rev. Fr. Bernard Laverty was made Parish Priest in Upper Mourne, he succeeded him as administrator of Saint Patrick's.

In 1930 Fr. O'Kelly purchased Ekenhead Presbyterian Church in North Queen Street and, after being blessing by the bishop, opened it as Saint Kevin's Chapel of Ease, though this has since been demolished with a parochial hall built in its place. He died in July 1933, at the age of fifty-four and was interred in Milltown Cemetery, having served as administrator of Saint Patrick's for a decade. His requiem Mass was performed by his first cousin, the Rev. Fr. Joseph Ivory, with the Most Rev. Daniel Mageean presiding.

Patrick McAlea

Born in McAleastown, Sheepland More, in 1901, the Rev. Fr. Pat McAlea developed, in his younger years, a keen passion for fishing off the rocks at Sheepland and was an able craftsman. He was ordained to the priesthood at the Irish College at Paris on 7 June 1923, celebrating his first Mass the following day and his final ordination was on the 7 December 1925 when he returned home. Between the years 1950 and 1960 he was the administrator at Saint Mary's, Chapel Lane, Belfast, in succession to the Rev. Fr. Daniel Gogarty.

Fr. Patrick McAlea. Photograph courtesy of Sean McAlea.

In the Marian year, 1954, after the Most Rev. Dr. Mageean granted permission, Fr. McAlea erected a grotto celebrating the Apparition of Our Lady of Lourdes and the Rev. Fr. John McKee was invited back to the chapel to celebrate High Mass. The shrine has been a focus of devotion in Belfast city centre ever since. The year 1957 was particularly poignant when Northern Ireland became home to Hungarian refugees escaping Russian repression after the rising in Budapest the previous year. They were invited to the procession, at which they carried a blood stained Hungarian flag, and afterwards the Rev. Fr. McAlea received a letter expressing gratitude from the refugees at Ballymacormick camp. There is also an art collection at Saint Mary's which includes a painting of the Sacred Heart by Willie Fee, a member of the Church of Ireland, which was given as a gift to Fr. Pat.

He then succeeded to the appointment of Parish Priest at Ballyphilip in 1960 and, before leaving in 1965, Fr. Pat purchased two shops and a house and, after an appeal for donations, acquired parts of a number of gardens to provide a site for the new Saint Cooey's Oratory. The oratory was completed in 1968 and, prior to its erection, Mass had been celebrated in Saint Patrick's Parish Hall. After leaving Portaferry, Fr. McAlea served as Parish Priest at Saint John's in Belfast. In 1971 he retired to Portaferry and Henry Fitzsimons recorded his death on 2 December 1972. The Rev. Fr. Pat McAlea was interred at Portaferry.

Catherine Killen

A grand-niece of the Reverend Fathers Killen and born at Tollumgrange in 1888, Catherine entered the Cross and Passion

Sr. Fina in the centre with her sisters, Cecilia Harte and Josephine Killen. Photograph courtesy of Bernadette Killen.

Convent at Ballycastle. When she took her religious vows, she assumed the religious name of the Sister Fina Joseph. She died on 11 January 1975 having worked for many years in the convent at Ballycastle.

Mary Ellen Milligan

Leaving Ardglass in 1935 at the age of twenty-two and entering the Order of Our Lady of the Apostles at Ardfoyle, County Cork, Mary Ellen took her final vows two years later in Rostrevor and was given the religious name of Sister Comgall. A keen musician, she became a licentiate of the London College of Music and trained religious and school choirs throughout her career.

Sr. Comgall. This photograph and information kindly provided by Michael Howland.

She spent a large part of her mission, thirty-eight years in fact, in Nigeria, west Africa and, whilst there, assisted those converting to Catholicism. She returned to Ardglass for a visit in August 1953 and held a function to raise funds for her mission in the Shield Memorial Hall, which was owned by her brother Gerry. Sister Comgall was well respected in her work and, throughout her whole mission, she worked closely with priests from the Society of African Missions who had founded her order. Whenever anything needed to be done, Sister Comgall was a great organiser who had numerous contacts in various ports and airports and this proved to be of great assistance to the missions.

She died on 26 September 1995, having devoted sixty years of her life to her order. The Rev. Fr. Kevin McGarry, whose family live in Ardglass, was the chief celebrant at her funeral which was held in Ardfoyle.

Elizabeth Anne Magee

As the youngest member of the Magee family of Chapeltown following the death of her sister, Elizabeth was sent to a boarding school in Portstewart. It was here that she first heard the call to her vocation in her younger teenage years. Later, at the age of eighteen, she made her first profession for the missionary novitiate at the Dominican convent at Tamnaharry, near Warrenpoint. Her widowed mother gave her wedding ring

Sr. Alvarez greeting Pope John Paul II. This photograph and information kindly provided by Alvarez Magee.

to Elizabeth for her profession. Taking the name of Sister Alvarez, she left by ship from Southampton for South Africa, having entered her mission in the knowledge that she would never be able to return home. The journey took three weeks and it was there that she spent sixty-three years on the mission, working for much of this time as a principal in various schools. She spent the first half of her mission in Newton Hague and Port Elizabeth and the second half in Capetown.

But during the Second Vatican Council, His Holiness Pope John XXIII decided to relax missionary principles and, for the first time in thirty-four years, Sister Alvarez was able to return home to Dunsford. Back in the mission field she worked closely with her home parish, raising funds to assist her friend, the Rev. Fr. Curran, in his A.I.D.S. hospitals. She worked secretly at night with many other sisters by going out into the townships to educate the inhabitants knowing full well that what she was doing was against the law during apartheid. Her death in Capetown on 26 December 1997, at the age of eighty-four, was recorded by Henry Fitzsimons and it was there that her remains were interred.

Margaret Angela Clinton

Born at Sheepland More in 1937, Margaret was the youngest child of Francis and Kathleen Clinton. For her secondary education she was sent to Saint Michael's in Lurgan as a boarder. She then enrolled at University College Dublin where she graduated with a B.A. in Maths, Latin, and History after three years of study. As a post graduate Margaret then entered Saint Mary's University, Belfast to undertake teacher training. After taking her final profession, she became a member of the Convent of the Sisters of Mercy in Lurgan, taking the name of Sister Angela. She entered Saint Michael's, the school where she had been a boarder, as a teacher and very soon was asked by the principal to replace her after retirement. Sister Angela herself retired in 1997, having fulfilled the role of principal of Saint Michael's for many years.

Marie Killen

The niece of Sister Fina Joseph Killen, Marie was born at Tullomgrange in 1937. At the age of seventeen, she joined the Dominicans at Kerdiffstown, county Kildare, in 1954. She was given the name of Sister Áine and dedicated much of her religious life to education, spending much of her time teaching in the Little Flower Secondary School on the Somerton Road in Belfast. Then, at the time

Sr. Aine. Photograph courtesy of Bernadette Killen.

of the Falklands war, she spent time in Argentina. Returning to Ireland, her pastoral work continued, firstly in Dublin and then in Galway, working with the travelling community. She is currently residing in Dublin.

Henry Casey

Born in Belfast in 1941 and raised in Ardglass, the Rev. Fr. Harry Casey was ordained at Saint Patrick's and Saint Colman's Cathedral, Newry, by the Most Rev. Dr. Eugene O'Doherty, Bishop of Dromore, on 20 February 1965, one of seventeen priests ordained that day for the Society of African Missions. His maternal aunt was Sister Comgall. The following day, which was a Tuesday, he was invited by the Rev. Fr. Canon McKee to celebrate his first Mass in Saint Nicholas', Ardglass. After completing his studies, Fr. Harry was assigned to missionary work in Nigeria, the same country where his aunt had worked, and was appointed to the Archdiocese of Lagos in October 1967. He worked mostly in the Ijebu area of the archdiocese and, when the diocese was divided and Ijebu-Ode was created in 1969, the Rev. Fr. Harry continued to work within the new jurisdiction. Whilst there, he served in various parishes – Ibonwon, Ijebu-Igbo and Iperu-Remo – and as administrator of the Cathedral Parish until 1976, at which time he returned to Ireland.

Between 1976 and 1982 he continued to support the parish of Dunsford and Ardglass, performing regular baptisms. Unable to return to the missions, he was appointed to various parishes in Down and Connor. He served in Saint Columba's, Ballyhackamore in East Belfast for eight years until 1991; in Greenville until 1994; in the parish of Saint Mary's on the Hill, Whitehouse until 1997 and eleven years in the parish of Lower Mourne at Ballymartin between 1997 and 2008. He passed away at the Downe Hospital aged sixty-six, and was interred at Ardglass.

Fr. Cross on the day he entered the Graan. Included, from left to right, are his father Tom, Bernadette Killen, who supplied the picture, Sue Doran, his sister Elsie, his mother Sheila, and his brother Martin.

Charles Cross

A native of Ross, the Rev. Fr. Charlie Cross was ordained in Saint Mary's in Chapeltown at a ceremony attended by more than three hundred people. He began his mission by joining the Juniorate of the John of God Brothers, before deciding to join the Order of Passionists. In 1970 he went to the Passionist Novitiate at the Graan in Enniskillen. After this he was based in Mount Argus, Dublin, where he studied philosophy and theology at the Milltown Institute. At his ordination by the Most Rev. Eugene Arthurs, Bishop of Tanga in Tanzania, the Reverend Fathers Patrick White and Eamonn Magee assisted the bishop, together with priests and brothers of the Passionist Order. Among those in attendance at the event were the Reverend Fathers Jim Skelly and Patsy McGarry, who would have known Charlie when he was a boy, and Fr. John Fitzpatrick who had recently left the parish.

Fr. Charlie, as a member of the Order of Passionists, which is a peripatetic vocation, ministers to an international congregation, meaning that he does not serve any diocese exclusively. Since his ordination he has worked on retreats throughout Ireland and was resident in many parts of the island. He also served in Africa. A main focus of his work was to provide spiritual retreats for priests and nuns. Since 2013 he has been working at Holy Cross church in Ardoyne in Belfast, and 2016 will mark forty years since Fr. Charlie's ordination in the parish.

Derek Kearney

A native of the townland of Sheepland More, the Rev. Fr. Derek Kearney joined the Society of African Missions and was ordained a deacon in Maynooth by Cardinal Cathal B. Brady in 1991, the year when Saint Mary's marked its bicentenary. On 28 June 1992 he was ordained in Saint Mary's in Chapeltown by the Most Rev. Dr. Anthony Farquhar, Auxiliary Bishop of Down and Connor, and a former Reader in the parish. In September of that year, Fr. Derek was sent to Nigeria where he learned the local language of Yoruba and officiated for two and a half years at Saint Agnes' in Lagos. For the next two years he was sent to the Formation House for the Society of African Missions where he assisted in the training of local men going through the seminary.

In 1997 he travelled across the Atlantic to America to study at Saint Louis University, Missouri, and in the following year travelled to Loyola University where he entered a Masters programme to further his role in the training of seminarians in Africa. From there he proceeded to the Ivory Coast to work in the seminary there, this time with French speakers, for a further two years until the new millennium. Following this appointment Fr. Kearney assumed the role of Superior of the Formation House in Zambia for a further four years.

Fr. Kearney returned to Ireland on a sabbatical which he spent in Dublin. Whilst there he attended All Hallows College, studying for a further Masters degree. Then, after working in Paris, he went to Rome where he was appointed Secretary General for the Society of African Missions. After working in this role for six years, he came back to Lecale to care for his father and, on Easter Sunday 2016, fulfilled an ambition to celebrate Mass at Struell Wells.

Author's note

Whilst the information compiled on these later biographies of those from the parish who spent many years on the mission field are as accurate and as comprehensive as possible, there remain curious references made by Richard Clark about two priests from the parish about whom little information has come to light. All we know is that the Rev. Fr. Joseph Fitzsimons died in Trinidad on 13 September 1849 and that the Rev. Fr. James Gilchrist returned home after eight years spent in Newfoundland on 16 November 1849.

TEN

Priests since 1791

I wish to pay my grateful thanks to George Rice without whose help I would not have been able to create this list. George has provided the dates of the successive appointments to the parish and I have embellished this information with a biography of each member of the clergy where possible.

Edward Mulholland P.P., 1789-1805

Appointed on 9 February 1789, the Rev. Fr. Edward Mulholland was a distinguished scholar and preacher. This remarkable man was the builder of the parish's first post Reformation chapel in 1791. For the two years prior to the building work, he had obviously spent a long time acquiring an extensive dossier of knowledge as to what should be included in the new chapel in terms of its antiquity. This was an extraordinary feat as he was not a native of the parish. The tablet in Saint Mary's was inscribed with his own hand. This short couplet is how he was recalled by the people who knew him:

> Mulholland's virtues trav'ler passing by
> Revere; reflect and ponder with a sigh.

When the French frigate, *L'Amitie*, sank off the rocks at Sheepland in April 1797, it is quite likely that Fr. Mulholland would have been called to the bedside of the steersman who was the sole survivor[56] of the crew of 104.

Fr. Mulholland's health deteriorated and he died on 25 July 1805. His obituary from the *Belfast Commercial Chronicle* reads, 'He was a learned and zealous pastor, an ornament of the order

---

[56] Of the crew that made it off the vessel all but one perished on the snowclad moors of Sheepland. The local inhabitants were terrified when they heard the plaintive cries in a foreign language, mistaking French for the cries of the Bean Sidhe. The following morning they went out to the site of a disaster but only found the steersman alive, huddled down between two sheep. He had a severe wound to his head and it seems likely that Fr. Mulholland would have been called upon to help him. And, to escape the attention of the government, the bodies of the sailors who had perished were hurriedly buried.

he belonged to, and an invaluable acquisition to the parish over which he ruled 17 years'. His epitaph reads:

Of years but few – yet full of merits rare
Here was a priest who while he breathed the air
His flock from foes infernal did defend
With zeal instruct them – did their morals mend
Whom all that knew – did reverence – fear and love
We hope in bliss he reigns with Saints above.
Edward Mulholland Dunsford never forget
In whom devotion with great learning met.

Eugene Mulholland P.P., 1805-1832

Eugene was appointed to the parish upon the death of his brother, the Rev. Fr. Edward, coming from Mourne parish where he had been acting as curate. The two boys had been raised in Drumgooland in the parish of Loughinisland, Eugene being five years younger than Edward. Initially Eugene followed a very different path from his brother before his call to the priesthood and only entered Maynooth in 1798. He was Parish Priest here when the ground on which Saint Nicholas' stands was granted. He passed away in his 68th year at his residence in Tollumgrange on 9 February 1832. The obituary in the *Newry Telegraph* reads, "for nearly 27 years he discharged with zeal and indefatigable assiduity the duties of a faithful and religious pastor."

John O'Heggarty C.C., 1827-1829

Ordained in 1816 by the Most Rev. Dr. Patrick MacMullan after serving as curate both in Ahoghill and then in Dunsford and Ardglass, the Rev. Fr. O'Heggarty, a native of Kilrea in County Derry, was appointed, from Dunsford and Ardglass, Parish Priest to Maghera (Bryansford). An enthusiastic and able cleric, he rebuilt the chapel at Bryansford in 1829, the year of his appointment. He was assigned to Armoy and Ballintoy on 25 March 1843. He died while Parish Priest of Ballymoney on 1 March 1853 (or 1852), aged 64, and was interred in Ballymoney church where the Pieta is located at the west end of the southern aisle of the new church. We are greatly indebted to Fr. O'Heggarty for all his hard work in the erection of Saint Nicholas' between May and November 1828.

Peter Denvir P.P., 1832-1848

After the death of Fr. Eugene Mulholland, the Rev. Fr. Peter Denvir was appointed Parish Priest and he remained in the parish for sixteen years. He was a native of Loughkeelan and born in 1783. He had previously served as a curate in Bright and was Parish Priest of Ballyphilip for a decade until he resigned in 1825 and took on the role of administrator at Blaris. After leaving Dunsford and Ardglass he was appointed Parish Priest at Bright on 30 January 1848.

He was the first Parish Priest to reside in Ardglass. Within months of taking up his parish duties, he found himself at the heart of the cholera epidemic which gripped the area from 26 July 1832, shortly after the second sailing of the ship *Harriet* which was plying between Ardglass and Liverpool. Fr. Denvir was appointed to the Board of Health and quite promptly a new field hospital was built to deal with the patients and like so many others he contributed to its erection. At the close of the epidemic forty four people were left destitute and in receipt of poor relief. Unlike his Anglican colleague, the Rev. George Crane[57], Fr. Denvir survived the epidemic. Responding to queries from Parliament four years later, MPs were informed that there were thirty widows and children in Ardglass still requiring the support of the people.

Fr. Denvir was also incumbent during the first years of the Great Famine. Richard Clark wrote, "in October 1845 potatoes in Ireland began to show symptoms of disease and continued so till May 1846 causing them to be scarce and dear." The effects of this

---

[57] Rev. George Crane's grave is the only known one from the epidemic and is to be found in the churchyard at Saint Nicholas' on Kildare Street.

were not greatly felt until the end of 1846 and on "January 7th 1847 Ardglass soup kitchen was opened in the Bann house for the benefit of the poor, by subscription, the Major giving £20 and others from 1s 0 to 6d each weekly."

We should be mindful that the Great Famine occurred during a recession and there are many accounts of people falling on hard times. "A general fast was kept and divine service was held in all the churches throughout the Kingdom on Wednesday 24th March 1847 by order in Parliament." The following day it was noted that Fr. Denvir was absent from Ardglass; in July he was unable to perform Mass, and in December he was again absent. He took his leave from the parish in January and "install[ed] Rev. Fr. Francis McKenny in his room." Whilst serving at Bright, he lived at The Bridge in Killough. He died suddenly following a fall from his horse on Course Hill in Downpatrick on 8 November 1855 and was buried in Chapeltown in accordance with his wishes. A few months later Richard Clark wrote:

> On Tuesday 4th March 1856 a Requiem, or High Mass, was celebrated in Killough Chapel for the happy repose of the late Priest Denvir. The whole got up by Priest MacMullan of Dunsford. The Bishop and a number of the clergy attended.

> Hic jacet
> In spem ressurectionis beatæ,
> Revdus Petrus Denver,
> Qui in hac parœcia de Dunsford,
> Ab anno MDCCCXXXII usque ad MDCCCXLVIII.
> Parochi munere functus est
> Deinceps usque ad obitium,
> Parœcia de Bright præfuit.
> Morum urbanitate insignis,

Animarum salute maxime studiosus

Caritate Catholica ardens.

Animos omnium sibi concilavit.

Diem obiit supremum VI Idus Novembris,

Ætatis suse anno LXXIII,

Salutis autem reparatæ MDCCCLV.

Requiescat in pace.

Priest Magee C.C., 1840s

There is reference to a priest officiating at the funeral of William Gilchrist's wife in March 1843, possibly James Magee[58].

Priest Taggart C.C., 1840s

The Rev. Fr. Taggart must have been curate to Rev. Fr. Denvir as he appears in the *Diary of Richard Clark* with reference to the marriage of Jane Ramsey and William Kurnod, a Manxman, on 30 September 1843 and again officiating at the marriage of Henry Gill and Anne Ramsey on 4 November 1843 at Henry Gill's own house. Then, in January 1845, he is found officiating at the marriage of John Conn of Tollumgrange, and Miss Napier of Ballybrannagh, in Mrs. Brown's premises, otherwise known as The Ardglass Arms.

Francis McKenny Acting P.P., 1848

Before his departure from the parish, the Rev. Fr. Denvir installed the Rev. Fr. Francis McKenny. He only remained for a short period until the Rev. Fr. William MacMullan "made his entry in Dunsford Chapel on Sunday 13th February 1848." Whilst this short period in the service of the parish may not seem remarkable, this man's career was. While Parish Priest of Drummaul, he officiated at a marriage between a Catholic and Protestant which in those days was a criminal offence. To escape the consequences he fled to the United States of America where he was a missionary for some years. There have been, however, a few interdenominational

---

[58] Reference 182, *A Digest of the historical account of the Diocese of Down and Connor.*

weddings in this parish, clearly demonstrating the good relations amongst all Christian traditions in the Lecale area.

William MacMullan P.P., 1848-1876

A native of Loughinisland, William was the third successive generation of clerics in his family and was handed the gauntlet of Dunsford and Ardglass in February 1848. His great uncle was the Most Rev. Dr. MacMullan, Bishop of Down and Connor, and his uncle the Rev. Fr. William MacMullan, Parish Priest of Loughinisland. William was appointed to this parish from Derriaghy where he had served since 1845. During his incumbency in this parish he resided at The Crescent, Ardglass. He was the priest who began the register of baptisms, marriages, and funerals in the parish and this is the reason why the collection for Dunsford and Ardglass, created by the National Library of Ireland, begins with Derriaghy.

During his tenure, there existed in Ardglass, like other places in Lecale, a strong temperance movement which, within one year, succeeded in convincing ten publicans to cease their trade. He carried on with the improvements at Saint Nicholas' and, in August 1851, had the pleasure of auctioning ten seats in front of the altar, selling them from between £10 and £16. Richard Clark's son, William, who continued the tradition of diary keeping, recorded "1876 died at Ardglass Father Wm McMullen PP of Dunsford aged 59 years." He was interred at Loughinisland in the same grave as his uncle and great uncle. In his will he bequeathed £65 to the poor of the parish and a further £15 for the education of the parish's poor children. It was noted by the Rev. Monsignor James O'Laverty that "a chalice in Dunsford Church has the inscription *Rev. Dr. Patrick MacMullan 1793*", but unfortunately this has since disappeared.

Richard Marner P.P., 1876-1885

The Rev. Dr. Richard Marner was born in the parish of Kilmore and was a professor of Classics and Mathematics in the Diocesan

College. Later he became president of the college and extended the curriculum considerably. He was granted a long leave of absence on health grounds and used this time to travel extensively through Italy, Greece, Egypt, Palestine and other countries in Europe and Asia. On 26 March 1876, he was appointed Parish Priest at Dunsford and Ardglass and immediately began a project allowing the influences from his travels to embellish Saint Nicholas'. In 1879 he added a porch, the sacristy, the semi-circular chancel and a sanctuary as well as the reredos screen behind the altar and the gallery. He also reordered Saint Mary's which is probably the reason that the church's sanctuary orientation is unusual as it is at the west end of the church.

Dr Marner was the grandnephew of the Rev. Fr. Richard Curoe, the last priest to officiate in Down and Connor worshipping under the canopy of heaven. His nephew went on to become the Most Rev. Dr. Daniel Mageean. In 1885 he was relocated to Upper Mourne. The church there, which at that time had been recently completed, also has a similar reredos to the one in Saint Nicholas' although this time it has Synagoga and Christ enthroned. He was short in stature hence the reason that both the altars in Ardglass and Massforth are low. In spite of his cold and unapproachable demeanour he was a very warm personable cleric. The familiar sight of his pony and trap was recalled for many years by the parish. He received two nominations for the bishopric of Down and Connor and was known by his priestly colleagues as 'Two Votes Marner'. William Clark recorded his death in 1906 – "March 4th at Kilkeel Father Marner D.D. P.P. formerly of Dunsford Parish." Having served the parish of Upper Mourne for over twenty years, his remains were interred at Massforth, Kilkeel.

Patrick Walsh C.C., 1870s

The Rev. Fr. Patrick Walsh was curate to Dr. Marner in the late 1870s, and it was he who baptised the Rev. Fr. Patrick O'Kelly.

William J. Walsh C.C., 1880-1881

The Rev. Fr. William Walsh was a curate on loan for a period of eight months from July 1880 to Dr. Marner from the Diocese of Waterford and Lismore. Returning to his native diocese, he later rose to the rank of Monsignor and was Dean of Saint Peter's and Saint Paul's in Clonmel. He was responsible for the completion of the church there between 1919 and 1934. He died the following year in 1935.

John Tohill C.C., 1881-1882

A native of Gortmacrane, near Kilrea, in the Parish of Tamlaght-O'Crilly, he succeeded Fr. Walsh and remained in this parish for thirteen months from March 1881 until April 1882. Before his curacy in Dunsford and Ardglass, he studied the classics in Saint Malachy's and entered Maynooth in 1875. He was made a professor in the Diocesan College in September 1878, before his ordination by the Most Rev. Dr. Patrick Dorrian. It was to this college that he returned in 1882. Following the death of the Most Rev. Dr. Henry Henry in 1908, he was consecrated the 26th Lord Bishop of Down and Connor on 20 September 1908. As Bishop of Down and Connor, he returned to this parish for the purpose of dedicating the grotto of Our Lady of Lourdes and died suddenly, shortly afterwards, on 4 July 1914.

J.J. Donnelly C.C., 1882-1885

The Rev. Fr. Donnelly succeeded Fr. Tohill as curate in April 1882 and remained as curate until 1885. He was a native of Magherafelt in County Derry and later returned to this parish as Parish Priest in 1898.

Edward Crawford P.P., 1885-1898

The Rev. Fr. Crawford was a native of Killough, born there in 1844. He had studied at Saint Malachy's, entering the Rhetoric Class at Maynooth in 1866.

"I was appointed to this parish on the 13th June 1885 and took charge on the 1st July of the same year, – E. Crawford P.P.." These words are inscribed at the bottom of the first page of the *Marriage Register of the Parish of Dunsford* which was begun the previous year, 1884.

He was ordained by the Most Rev. Dr. Dorrian in February 1872, at the Diocesan College. His first appointment was as curate to Loughinisland and shortly afterwards he assumed the same role at Kilmore. Later he became administrator at Saint Patrick's,

Fr. Edward Crawford. Photograph from Fitzsimons family collection.

Belfast, the parish which he was serving when he was offered Dunsford and Ardglass. When the Rev. Fr. Edward Connor declined the role of Parish Priest Fr. Crawford accepted. He continued development at Ardglass where he built the parochial house in 1886, the year after his appointment. William Clark records under deaths "1898 October 19th at Ardglass suddenly Father Crawford aged 54 years offering £35.0.0." He was interred at Rossglass.

Patrick McCambridge C.C., 1885-1887

The Rev. Fr. Patrick McCambridge was curate to Fr. Crawford for two years from 25 July 1885 until July 1887. He was born in 1852 at Ranaghan, Duneane near Toome. He proceeded to the Irish College in Paris where he entered the Logic Class and was ordained there by the Most Rev. Dr. Fitzgerald, Bishop of Ross, in 1878. Prior to his arrival in this parish, he had served as curate in the Parish of Ballykinlar for four years. Before being appointed as Parish Priest to Bright in 1906, he had worked in Drumaroad as Parish Priest. He died in July 1925 having been incumbent at Bright for nineteen years.

Anthony Gallagher C.C., 1887-1889

Fr. McCambridge's successor, the Rev. Fr. Anthony Gallagher came on loan from the Diocese of Raphoe and remained for two years. During his time as curate in Dunsford and Ardglass, between July 1887 and August 1889, he appears to have performed more marriage ceremonies than the Parish Priest, Fr. Crawford. He returned to Raphoe as curate at Killybegs and later served on Arranmore Island where his work for the fishermen is fondly remembered to this day. Undoubtedly some of his parishioners would have worked on the boats at the harbour at Ardglass. Before becoming Parish Priest in Glenfin in 1913, he worked in Gweedore. He died at the age of sixty-three in October 1926.

Denis O'Brien C.C., 1889-1893

The successor to Fr. Gallagher who remained for almost four years between August 1889 and July 1893, was the Rev. Fr. O'Brien who had come on loan from the Diocese of Kerry. In 1911 he was curate at Coomlogane and later, in 1920, he was working in the parish of Cahirciveen as Parish Priest and Prior.

Hugh Fitzpatrick C.C., 1893-1897

The Rev. Fr. Hugh Fitzpatrick was appointed curate in July 1893 and stayed until July 1897. The 1901 census reveals that he was working as a curate in Randalstown and living in Ballygrooby townland. William Clark's diary records his death, "1905 January 6th at Aughnahoary, Kilkeel, Father Hugh Fitzpatrick formerly a curate in Dunsford Parish R.I.P." He would have died around the age of forty and Dunsford and Ardglass had been his first curacy.

David J. McWilliams C.C., 1897-1899

Born in the parish of Saint Peter's Belfast in 1871, the Rev.

Fr. McWilliams entered Saint Malachy's College and proceeded to the Theology Class in Maynooth in August 1891. He was ordained by the Most Rev. Dr. Walsh, Archbishop of Dublin, on 24 August 1895. His first appointment was to Rathlin Island that same year and two years later he succeeded Fr. Fitzpatrick as curate to Dunsford and Ardglass where he remained until August 1899. He went on to become an Archdeacon when he was Parish Priest in Downpatrick.

Archdeacon David J. McWilliams. Photograph from the Fitzsimons family collection.

He returned in 1960 to open the new Saint Mary's Primary School. It may appear odd that he should return so many years later for this purpose but the fact is that Canon McWilliams was a staunch advocate for the improvement of education for Catholics. In Downpatrick alone in Downpatrick alone he had helped with the building of five schools; Saint Patrick's, De La Salle, Saint Mary's, Saint Patrick's Boys and Convent of Mercy Girls. So strident was he with the Education Board that, when he died on 27 October 1960, a telephone call came through to the parochial house in Downpatrick asking for him and, when informed that he had died, the person on the other end of the phone replied, 'Are you sure!?'

Before his long service at Downpatrick he had acted as Parish Priest in Newcastle between 1917 and 1933. In 1935 he built the Canon's Hall in Downpatrick, a building synonymous with many social functions attended by those throughout the district during the 1950s and 1960s.

J.J. Donnelly P.P., 1899-1927

Having previously served as a curate at Dunsford fourteen years previously, the Rev. Fr. Donnelly returned in 1899 as Parish Priest. He was the incumbent at the time of the recovery of Our Lady of Dunsford and would have previously been made aware of the existence of the statue by Dr. Marner. At the auction of Ardglass, he purchased the church and parochial house. And, in that same year, a man of great ornament came to reside in his newly restored home, Jordan's Castle. That was F.J. Bigger. Canon Donnelly presided over the parish during the Gaelic Revival which was invigorated by F.J. Bigger's efforts and the two men became great friends.

Canon Donnelly died on 11 June 1927, leaving money to ensure that a Celtic cross would be erected over his grave at the front of Saint Nicholas'. Priests from a wide area and in large numbers attended the funeral which was presided over by the Most Rev. Dr. MacRory. Many touching references were made in all the other churches in Ardglass on the occasion of the Canon Donnelly's passing.

Rose Mulhall, in her memoir, writes of the chapel and the Canon:

Opposite Mc Nallys was The R C Church and up the tree lined avenue was the Priests house, to be caught climbing trees in this sacred ground called for punishment and our Canon Donnelly didnt spare the rod.

He owned one of the two cars in the village — No High way code for him, he put the boot down, and kept the horn on — so when the local children heard the horn. They ran for cover, and the hens on the street flew in all directions

Denis McCartan C.C., 1899-1902

Born in Newcastle upon Tyne on 9 September 1874 to parents from Castlewellan, the Rev. Fr. McCartan was appointed to the curacy of Dunsford and Ardglass in November 1899 and remained until January 1902. His family returned to Castlewellan where his parents opened the Mourne View Bar, next to the entrance to the Annesley Estate. In 1908 Fr. McCartan installed a stained glass window in memory of his parents at Saint Malachy's in Castlewellan. In 1911 he was serving in Belfast and later, in 1920, he was curate at Saint Pauls', Belfast. After enjoying a long vocation of over sixty years and rising to the post of Canon, he passed away on 12 November 1965, at the age of ninety-one, when he was Parish Priest of Randalstown.

Canon Donnelly with Fr. Denis McCartan (standing) and Fr. O'Brien, a missionary priest. Photograph from the Fitzsimons family collection.

James Greene C.C., 1902-1904

The Rev. Fr. Greene was appointed as curate to Fr. Donnelly in January 1902 and stayed until early 1904. Fr. Greene appears to have only ever officiated at one wedding during his time here. Later in his career he officiated as Parish Priest at Ballygalget from 1942 until 1955.

Patrick Bradley C.C., 1904-1907

The Rev. Fr. Bradley enjoyed a three and a half year tenure as curate in Dunsford and Ardglass from 1904 until December 1907. Like Fr. Donnelly, he was a native of Derry and was proficient in the Irish language. Both were popular priests who seemed to have had a good working relationship, sharing equally the number of marriages. Fr. Donnelly even bore witness at the marriage of Bob Connolly of Sheepland to Minnie Fitzsimons, on 24 June 1906 which had been performed by Fr. Bradley. Whilst in Chapeltown he took a keen interest in the education of children in the

Canon Donnelly with Fr. Ambrose, missionary of the Order of Passionists, and Fr. Patrick Bradley.

National School where he presented a book to the author's great grandmother, Maggie Clinton, for excellent exam results.

After leaving Dunsford and Ardglass, he served as curate for many years in other parishes before becoming Parish Priest at Saint Vincent de Paul, Ligoniel, from 1931 to 1934. Afterwards he was appointed to Carnlough for nine years until 1943. The Rev. Fr. Patrick Bradley died whilst Parish Priest at Duneane where he had served until his death in 1950.

Patrick McNamara C.C., 1907-1909

The Rev. Fr. McNamara was a native of County Leitrim and was appointed curate here in December 1907, remaining until August 1909. He then became curate to the Rev. Fr. James Kennedy, native of this parish, in the Parish of Antrim in 1911. In 1914 he was subsequently appointed curate to Glenavy and then in 1920 transferred as curated to the Rev. Fr. James O'Boyle in the parish of Ballymoney and Derrykeighan. In an odd twist of fate, he once again succeeded Fr. Patrick Bradley for a second time when he was appointed Parish Priest of Saint Vincent de Paul, Ligoniel, where he served from 1934 to 1948, a period which included the Belfast Blitz.

James B. Murray C.C., 1909-1911

Born in County Antrim, the Rev. Fr. Murray served a short curacy in Dunsford and Ardglass from August 1909 until March 1911. After leaving this parish, he was appointed to the curacy at Lisburn where his name is found in the census at the parochial house in Longstone Street, aged 28. He is later found, in 1920, acting as curate to Rev. Fr. J.K. O'Neill at Sacred Heart in Belfast.

W.D. Byrne C.C., 1911-1916

The Rev. Fr. Byrne, another native of County Antrim, was successor to the Rev. Fr. Murray in April 1911 and remained here until March 1916. In 1920 he was performing the role of curate to Maghera.

James Murphy C.C., 1916-1920

The Rev. Fr. Murphy served as curate to Dunsford and Ardglass from March 1916 until October 1920. However his records after this period remain elusive.

Daniel Gogarty C.C., 1920-1922

The Rev. Fr. Gogarty was curate at Dunsford and Ardglass from October 1920 until August 1922. In 1942 he succeeded the Rev. Fr. John McKee as administrator of Saint Mary's in Belfast and in 1950 he was appointed Parish Priest to Dundrum where he remained until his move to Kilkeel in 1963. Henry Fitzsimons entered in his diary on 26 October 1975 the following words, "Canon Gogarty of Kilkeel, formerly curate in Dunsford, died." Having been in the ministry for well over fifty years, Canon Gogarty was yet another priest who had served his first curacy in this parish.

Michael McLoughlin C.C., 1922-1923

The Rev. Fr. McLoughlin, a native of Kilcoo, was appointed as curate to Fr. Donnelly in November 1922 and remained for over a year until December 1923. He had previously served as a curate in Blaris in 1920. In 1941 he became Parish Priest of Rasharkin following in the footsteps of a great uncle. He died in that parish on 23 August 1959, having been a priest for about fifty years.

James J. McConnell P.P., 1923-1925

The Rev. Fr. McConnell's curacy in Dunsford and Ardglass began in December 1923 and ended in February 1925. Previously he had served in Antrim as curate and later he was appointed Parish Priest to the Braid for a decade between 1933 until 1943. Subsequently he continued his ministry as Parish Priest of Dunloy until 1951.

William Lynn C.C., 1925-1931

Ordained at Maynooth in 1921 by the Most Rev. Dr. Byrne, Bishop of Spigaz, the curacy of the Rev. Fr. Lynn in this parish began in

February 1925. He had come from the neighbouring Parish of Kilclief where he had served since 1923. His was the first of the longer curacies in the parish's modern history, lasting for six years and ending in August 1931. Born in the United States of America in Chicago, Illinois, Fr. Lynn came to Ireland at the age of nine and never lost his American accent. He was the last curate to update the *Marriage Register for Dunsford and Ardglass* which ended when he took leave of the parish. Whilst serving as curate here, he worked both for Canon Donnelly and Fr. McNamee.

On leaving the parish he worked as curate in Ballyphilip and stayed there for eight years until 1939. He then transferred to Blaris and, in 1956, to Saint Matthew's, Belfast. Two years later in his mission he was appointed to the Parish of Saul in 1958. Whilst at Saul, the parish was the hive of activity on Saul Sunday when Mass was said on Slieve Patrick in August 1961 and the crowds on that day numbered thirty thousand people. Fr. Lynn died at Saul on 13 October 1971.

Bernard McNamee P.P., 1927-1942

A native of County Derry, the Rev. Fr. Bernard McNamee was appointed Parish Priest following the death of Canon Donnelly in 1927 and this was to be his only appointment as Parish Priest. Early records for Fr. McNamee have proved elusive although he was recorded as a curate at Dundrum and Tyrella in 1902 and later at Saint Paul's in Belfast in 1914, where he still was in 1920. He suffered from spoonerism, a speech impediment which meant that he could become muddled in his sentences. When Saint Mary's caught fire before Christmas in 1931, he appointed Pádraic Gregory, who holidayed at Ardglass, to arrange for the repair of the building.

In Ardglass Fr. McNamee continued improvements, having pillars built by Tommy Rooney and gates, made by H. Austin of Belfast, hung at the front to frame the Lourdes grotto. The gates have been replaced and the grotto is, of course, now gone, although the pillars remain. C.S. Pinkerton electrified the church in 1937. In 1940 the army requisitioned Saint Mary's parochial hall which they retained until the end of the war.

Whilst in charge of the parish Fr. McNamee clearly felt and appreciated the adverse effects and the devastation caused by the Belfast Blitz in 1941. Unlike London and other cities in Great Britain, there was no compulsory evacuation of children in Northern Ireland. However there was a voluntary scheme encouraged by the Northern Ireland government and Fr. McNamee responsibly encouraged as many of his parishioners as possible to take in evacuees and help provide for their education. Those families who had summer residences in Ardglass made a permanent home there, including one at Ardtole in which Canon Sean Rogan's family lived. In the early years of the war, Fr. McNamee was also responsible for tending to the spiritual needs of the Italian prisoners of war camped at Ballyhornan. He died on 9 May 1942 and was interred at the front of Saint Nicholas', Ardglass, next to his fellow countyman, Canon Donnelly.

Thomas O'Hare C.C., 1931-1937

The Rev. Fr. Thomas O'Hare served as curate to Fr. McNamee for almost six years from August 1931 until May 1937. Six years later he was appointed Parish Priest to Saint Patrick's, the Braid, where he remained until his retirement in 1957. He lived there for a further fourteen years until his death on 28 September 1971.

Patrick McDowell C.C., 1937-1941

The Rev. Fr. Patrick McDowell was curate from May 1937 until August 1941 and is remembered for keeping an Irish wolfhound as his canine companion. Fr. McDowell, who was an extremely learned man was, for many years, chaplain to the Christian Brothers on the Glen Road in Belfast. He remained a constant visitor to the area having struck up a friendship with Paddy Crangle of Ardtole. He passed away on 4 April 1988 at Helen's Bay.

Maurice McHenry C.C., 1941-1955

Hailing from Ballinlea in County Antrim, the Rev. Fr. McHenry's curacy is the longest in the modern history of the parish, lasting for fourteen years from August 1941 until September 1955. He studied at Queen's University Belfast and Maynooth, being ordained in 1939. His first appointment was as assistant priest to the ailing Canon William Murphy in the Parish of Kilmore for two years. His salary was very meagre and, as a result, he was taken in by the Flanagan family.

He arrived in the parish just one year before the Rev. Fr. John McKee. Shortly after his appointment to the parish, the immense Bishop's Court aerodrome was constructed by the R.A.F. and he became the first chaplain. Both he and Fr. McKee had a good rapport and an excellent working relationship. During the Corpus Christi procession, Fr. McHenry performed the role of master of ceremonies.

After leaving Dunsford and Ardglass, he was appointed curate to Waterfoot, remaining there for eleven years until his appointment as Parish Priest to Ahoghill in 1966. He was visiting

A young Monsignor Sean Connolly with his uncle Fr. Maurice McHenry. Photograph provided by Mairead Gilchrist, niece of the latter.

Dunsford and Ardglass again in 1970 when Fr. John Fitzpatrick was instituting changes in accordance with the Second Vatican Council's guidelines. Discovering that the green and white marble altar had been dismantled, he took the tabernacle away with him and relocated it in Saint Mary's at Ahoghill, where it remains to this day.

In June 1972 he became Parish Priest of Bright and the Rev. Fr. George McLaverty was his curate. Having suffered for many years from diabetes, Fr. McHenry's vision diminished. His former housekeeper, Maggie McKinney, who was from Redcastle in County Donegal, came back to look after him in his final years.

He passed away suddenly at the age of sixty-two in Killough on 9 January 1975.

John McKee P.P., 1942-1965

In spite of being a native of Loughguile, in County Antrim, the Rev. Fr. McKee played for both the Down hurling and football teams. He entered Saint Malachy's as a boarder in 1903, graduating six year later as a Bachelor of Arts. After ordination at Maynooth in 1913 by the Most Rev. Dr. Walsh, Archbishop of Dublin, he was appointed curate at Kilclief, and whilst there he transformed the hurling team. There is humorous anecdote about him recorded in *Lé Croí is Lámh*. He was claiming ignorance about the game when he took the hurl and drove the slíotar a considerable distance, thus letting it be known that he was, in truth, skilled at the game. In 1917 Fr. McKee transferred to Kilkeel, in 1926 to Sacred Heart, in 1930 to Saint Patrick's Belfast, and in 1938 to Saint Mary's Chapel Lane.

Before his arrival at Saint Mary's around the outbreak of the Second World War, it was discovered that the church, erected by Fr. Patrick Clarke, a native of Dunsford and Ardglass, in 1868, was in dire need of repair with deteriorating foundations. Fr. McKee set about the repair work just as the rationing of materials began. This seriously affected the work schedule which was then further delayed by the Belfast Blitz. But the work was completed with the solemn reopening of the reordered church, which survived unscathed during the war years. On entering Saint Mary's, one is struck by the beauty of the apse, the altar, and its mosaic, all built by Fr. McKee to the designs of Pádraic Gregory, all evidence of his classic religious taste.

He was appointed Parish Priest to Dunsford and Ardglass on 1 July 1942. An ardent revivalist and a zealous builder, Fr. McKee's contributions to the parish are recalled to this day. The state of educational provision was always of the utmost importance to him.

Canon McKee with his sister Sr. Agnes taken in South Africa. All four of the McKee sisters entered the Cross and Passion Order. Photograph from Margaret Gill's collection with thanks to Maureen Gill-Sharp.

He rebuilt Saint Joseph's Primary School at Ardglass, acquired a new site for Saint Mary's in Dunsford, and established Saint Anne's Intermediate School, raising the funds with neighbouring parishes of Kilclief and Bright. He always kept an affinity with his previous parishes and even returned to Belfast for the blessing of Saint Mary's Primary School in 1960.

In addition to his interest in education, he raised the necessary funds for the purchase of King's Castle from the Belfast Co-operative Society, re-establishing it as Mount Saint Clement's, a Redemptorist Retreat House. A man with many religious contacts, he invited numerous clergy to Ardglass to celebrate the first annual Corpus Christi celebration in 1950 with his friend, the Most Rev. Hugh Boyle, then the Vicar Apostolic of Port Elizabeth, leading the procession. When the Most Rev. Dr. William Philbin celebrated his golden jubilee in 1963, the town was decorated with flags and bunting which were sold at Charles Mulhall's shop. In the January of the following year, 1964, he was appointed a Canon.

On Sunday 7 February 1965, Canon McKee introduced the new Mass rite and, for the first time, celebrated the divine mysteries facing his assembled congregation. When his health began to fail, the recently ordained Rev. Fr. Anthony Farquhar, acting as Reader, assisted him. Canon John McKee died, just before Christmas, on 22 December 1965 at the Downe Hospital. In his twenty-three year tenure at Dunsford and Ardglass "he [had] won respect and affection by his pastoral zeal, leadership, and his warm personal qualities."[59]

Patrick McGarry C.C., 1955-1959

The Rev. Fr. Patsy McGarry, who later became a Canon, was appointed as curate to Fr. McKee and arrived in the parish on 16 September 1955. He remained in Dunsford and Ardglass for four years until August 1959. Whilst in the parish, Fr. McGarry identified with the needs of the people of Dunsford. When he saw the row of bicycles lying along the bank at Church Road each Sunday, he decided to raise funds to purchase a bus to bring the people to Mass. In addition to this, he was the man responsible for the present form of Saint Patrick's Well, having recruited volunteers from the parish to build the wall in 1958. The crucifix was donated to him by Fr. Pat McAlea who sent it from Saint Mary's in Chapel Lane. The site was once again at the centre of devotions, with rosaries being said on Sundays. He also brought a great social revival to the parish in the form of the annual Ballyhornan sports day.

---

[59] From the report of the jubilee in the *Irish Independent*.

Having been raised in the Parish of Kirkinriola in Ballymena, Fr. McGarry's first appointment as Parish Priest was to Randalstown in 1980. He remained there until 1988 when he was appointed to Duneane and, whilst there, he extended and altered Saint Oliver Plunkett's, Toomebridge. In 1996 he was appointed as first Parish Priest to Kilwee and, with the parish still in its infancy, he preached in a building which had previously served as a Presbyterian church on the Stewartstown Road. In 1999 he built Our Lady Queen of Peace, "an invocation chosen to further the cause of peace and reconciliation in Northern Ireland. ... He had the distinction of building three churches in three different parishes."[60] These were in Kilwee, at Saint Oliver Plunket's and, whilst still curate, completing the bombed Church of the Resurrection on the Cavehill Road. Sadly, Canon McGarry died just four months after the dedication of Our Lady Queen of Peace on 24 February 2000.

James Skelly C.C., 1959-1966

The Rev. Fr. James Skelly, born in Dublin in 1930, was appointed curate to Fr. McKee in August 1959, coming to this parish from Bangor. Having studied at Queen's University Belfast, he entered Maynooth and is remembered fondly by members of the parish as a kindly man. When he was curate, he would treat his altar servers to trips to Belfast as a token of gratitude. During the last year of his mission here, he worked with the Rev. Fr. Anthony Farquhar who had

Fr. Jim Skelly on the day of his ordination, from the Fitzsimons family collection.

---

[60] Page 24, *Down and Connor – A Short History.*

come to assist Canon McKee, with both men steering the parish after the Canon's demise. Fr. Skelly left in September 1966 when he was appointed curate to the parish of Coleraine. Subsequently, when the New University of Ulster was created there in 1968, he was appointed its chaplain. This was the year of marked change for Northern Ireland and at the outbreak of the Troubles, Fr. Jim Skelly's was a voice "articulating faith in a time of turmoil."

> And then in December 1975, Jim Skelly's gifts of outreach were given fresh, wider territory for action, when he accepted an invitation to join the religious programmes department in BBC Belfast, then headed by the very able and forward-looking Presbyterian, the Rev. Moore Wasson. He very soon earned the regard of colleagues at all levels and in all areas of broadcasting, socially as well as professionally – there are stories of convivial evenings in Sandy Row where the priest was an honoured and welcome guest. And his outstanding professional qualities were recognised when, on Moore Wasson's retirement, he became the obvious successor as departmental head – an appointment running counter to many of our perceived opinions about the North. His direct association with the BBC lasted until 1990 when, having reached the statutory age of 60, he retired[61].

He passed away on the 5 July 2000 at the age of 69. Requiem Mass was celebrated at Saint Colmcille's Church on the Upper Newtownards Road. The congregation was a mix of all sorts "priests, fishermen, bishops, broadcasters, former students, public faces, private friends and family – brought together by a common bond of affection for a remarkable and lovable man." His remains

---

[61] Obituary entitled "Broadcaster and visionary who tried to change northern society", *Irish Times*, 15 July 2000.

were afterwards brought to Ardglass for burial in the graveyard behind Saint Nicholas'.

Anthony Farquhar, Reader, 1965-1966

The Most Rev. Dr. Anthony Farquhar's first appointment, after ordination on 13 March 1965, was to Dunsford and Ardglass in September 1965. He came to assist the ailing Canon McKee and remained until March 1966. Though his tenure in Dunsford and Ardglass was short, he took on the full duties of the parish upon the death of Canon McKee. He was ordained Auxiliary Bishop of Down and Connor at the same time as Dr. Patrick Walsh, on 15 May 1983. As an auxiliary bishop of Down and Connor, he served thirty-two years, the longest tenure of any Catholic bishop. The Archbishop of Armagh, the Most Rev. Dr. Eamon Martin, praised him on his retirement in 2015 with these words, "His engagement and work with our fellow Christian denominations, especially during the Troubles, was of enormous support to sustaining the nascent peace process. I know that the leaders of the other Christian traditions greatly esteem his work for unity."

William B. Tumelty P.P., 1966-1967

Appointed on 1 March 1966, the Rev. Fr. Tumelty's tenure as Parish Priest was the shortest, ending in July 1967. Soon after his appointment to the parish, he celebrated Mass on Slieve Patrick on 5 June 1966. Obviously motivated by the recent recommendations of the Second Vatican Council in the previous year, he had major plans afoot for alterations to Saint Nicholas'. However he was appointed to Coleraine before he had the chance to put them into action and only the external painting was undertaken. Another sign of the modern thinking of this cleric may be seen in that he was the first priest to use correction fluid on his sermon notes.

During his career he was also a teacher at the Diocesan College. On leaving Coleraine in 1978, he was moved as Parish Priest to Kirkinriola (Ballymena) and, at the same time, was appointed a Vicar General and Domestic Prelate. When Saint John Paul II visited Ireland in 1979, the Reverend Monsignors Tumelty and Mullally were invited to represent the Diocese of Down and Connor, with Monsignor Tumelty leading the Prayers of the Faithful. In June 1989 he celebrated the golden jubilee of his ordination at Maynooth, retiring shortly afterwards but still continuing to act as curate to the parish. He passed away on 15 December 1992.

John J. Fitzpatrick C.C., 1966-1975

Appointed in September 1966, the Rev. Fr. Fitzpatrick was given free rein at Dunsford to enact the recommendations of the Second Vatican Council which had been granted in 1970. The marble altar, erected just over twenty years previously, was removed. During further renovations, which lasted around a year, the old National School was used for celebration of the Mass. Fr. Fitzpatrick remained in the parish until 13 March 1975 when he became curate at Whitehouse.

Patrick White P.P., 1967-1980

Appointed Parish Priest to Dunsford and Ardglass in September 1967, the Rev. Fr. Patrick White enacted the reordering of Saint Nicholas' by having the whole building replastered and new seating put in place. His efforts were less zealous than his curate's and thus Ardglass retained much of the work put in place by Canon McKee for another few years. Previously he had served in the Parish of Holy Family as an administrator and had been secretary of the Saint Patrick's Catholic Orphan Society. He remained in this parish until his appointment to Castlewellan in 1980. He retired in 1988 and is remembered as a passionate preacher, known for thumping the pulpit. He enjoyed a long retirement and passed away on 4 February 1999.

Eamonn Magee C.C., 1975-1987

Hailing from Downpatrick, the Rev. Fr. Magee was appointed curate to Fr. White in March 1975 and remained in the parish until 9 December 1987. Initially Fr. Magee was a Columban Father before becoming incardinated by the Diocese of Down and Connor. Pat Fitzsimons, who was at that time teaching up in Belfast, used the school's bus to help Father Magee move to his new rural parish. After leaving, he became Parish Priest in Drumaroad and Clanvaraghan, a post he held for two years until 1989. He retired to Dundrum and Tyrella and died on 11 July 2002.

John McAteer P.P., 1980-1985

The Rev. Fr. John McAteer was born in County Antrim. He was appointed as Parish Priest to Dunsford and Ardglass in October 1980. A lover of sport, he liked to play a wide range of activities, from hurling, to playing Gaelic football, or to having a round of golf. He is remembered for attending to the needs of his parishioners on his bicycle.

Fr. McAteer died whilst incumbent as Parish Priest on Holy Thursday, 4 April 1985. Before

Fr. John McAteer. Photograph from the Fitzsimons family collection.

arriving in this parish, he had succeeded Fr. Maurice McHenry as Parish Priest of Bright. During his forty-two year career, he had previously served the same parish as a curate and had earlier been curate of Saul and Ballee. Fr. McAteer's remains were interred at Saint Nicholas' on Easter Sunday.

Liam Mullan P.P., 1985-1990

The Rev. Fr. Mullan, a native of Coleraine born in June 1918, was appointed Parish Priest shortly after the death of Fr. McAteer, arriving in Ardglass on 31 May 1985. Educated at the Diocesan College, Queen's University Belfast and Maynooth, he was ordained by the Most Rev. Dr. Mageean in June 1943. His first appointment was to act as chaplain to the convent in Ballymena, going on to become curate. He continued to act in this role at Saint Joseph's, in Sailortown, and then at Saint Bernadette's in Belfast. Before his arrival as Parish Priest, he had been serving at Saint Luke's, Belfast, in the same role as Parish Priest from 1977 until to his appointment to our parish. Under Fr. Mullan the church began to implement the final stages of the Second Vatican Council including the introduction of the first Pastoral Council.

When he served at Twinbrook, he constructed a church raised from a foundation stone which had been blessed by Saint John Paul II at Knock. He remained until August 1990 when he was appointed Parish Priest at Portstewart where he remained until 1993, when he retired. He then briefly served in the Parish of Kilmore as curate and then lived for a decade as Priest in Residence at Saint Luke's where he passed away on the 30 December 2003. He was buried at Twinbrook.

Owen Reid C.C., 1987-1988

The Rev. Fr. Reid briefly performed the duties as curate for just over two months from 11 December 1987 until 26 February 1988 before returning to Belfast. Fr. Reid was unable to drive and found the rural nature of the parish difficult. In 1996 he was acting in the role of curate to the Parish of Maghera.

John J. Fitzpatrick C.C., 1988-1990

Coming as curate to Fr. Mullan, Fr. Fitzpatrick returned to the parish on 27 February 1988, becoming the second priest to have served twice in this parish. He remained until 25 August 1990 when he left to become Parish Priest of Rasharkin. He is now retired and resides in Seahornan and occasionally officiates at Masses in the parish.

Conleth Byrne P.P., 1990-2000

As successor to Fr. Liam Mullan, the Rev. Fr. Byrne was appointed on 25 August 1990, having come from the Parish of Kilmore where he had been serving since 1985. A native of Holy Rosary Parish in Belfast, he studied at the Diocesan College, Queen's University Belfast, and Maynooth and was ordained on 21 June 1959. His first appointment was as chaplain to Nazareth Lodge, before becoming a Reader in Upper Mourne, a chaplain at Helen's Bay, serving in Glasdrummond, and a curate in Antrim before coming to Kilmore.

He remained in Dunsford and Ardglass until 2000 when he was appointed Parish Priest at Loughinisland. During his incumbency here, both he and the Rev. Fr. McLaverty introduced eucharistic ministers to the parish by appointing eighteen of them in May 1992. The role, the reintroduction of an ancient practice, had been authorised by the Vatican in 1973 and this has facilitated the church in its modernisation. Fr. Byrne retired in 2010.

George McLaverty C.C., 1990-2002

The Rev. Fr. George McLaverty was appointed to the parish in August 1990 as curate to Fr. Byrne. Since 1988 he had been performing the duties of Parish Priest to Saint Mary's, Star of the Sea, Whitehouse. Fr. George's curacy which was one of the longest in the parish's history. Earlier in his career he had been curate to Fr. Maurice McHenry at Bright, residing at Legamaddy. A man with a clear passion for animals, he kept a goat there and during his time in Dunsford he kept his long-lived companion Rory, his Labrador, which everyone still remembers. And he always visited Galway for the horse races. He was a keen speaker of the Gaeilge language, ensuring that the pupils at Saint Mary's Primary School always greeted him in Irish.

During his time here, Saint Mary's Chapeltown marked its bicentenary and was substantially reordered. The number of rural parishioners in his pastoral care rapidly increased in 1993 when R.A.F. Bishop's Court closed and the houses were sold. His brother, Anthony, also served in the priesthood and would have, on occasion, celebrated Masses at Dunsford. On leaving Dunsford and Ardglass, he served at Saul before spending a few years in Downpatrick. Having been ordained in June 1964, Fr. George celebrated his golden jubilee in 2014 and has since retired.

Robert Fleck P.P., 2000-2013

Raised in Larne, the Rev. Fr. Robert Fleck's ordination in 1979 was the first to take place at Saint MacNissi's. He then went, in 1981, to Rome to study for a licentiate in Fundamental Theology. His first appointment was as chaplain to a number of different hospitals and this was followed by a few years teaching at St MacNissi's College at Garron Tower. Fr. Fleck then decided to continue his studies and returned to Rome to study Canon Law, matriculating with a doctorate five years later.

On return to the diocese, he worked briefly at Saint John's Parish on the Falls Road before taking up a role in the presbytery of Saint Patrick's, Donegall Street. Whilst there, he also acted as chaplain at the Mater Hospital. He was working in the parish of Saint Anne's in Dunmurry until 2000 when he was appointed successor to Fr. Byrne as Parish Priest of Dunsford and Ardglass.

Shortly after his arrival, Fr. Fleck began plans to remodel Saint Nicholas'. He undertook this momentous task in 2005, under the professional guidance of the architects, Donnelly O'Neill, one of whose architects on the project, Paul McMahon, actually knew Fr. Fleck when he was a boy and who later returned to the chapel to be married. As part of this work the graveyard was extended and the parochial house renovated. By this time the parish had no curate and so a committee was formed in Dunsford to decide whether the restoration of Saint Mary's should proceed. The decorative style of the 1991 renovation was curtailed enhancing the simplicity of the chapel's barn plan. In 2013, the Rev. Fr. Fleck was appointed as Parish Priest of Tyrella and Dundrum.

Gordon McKinstry C.C., 2002-2003

Ordained in 1965 and appointed curate to Fr. Fleck for a brief period, the Rev. Fr. McKinstry was the last curate to reside in Dunsford. Prior to his arrival here, he had served the Rev. Canon Noel Conway as curate in Kilclief.

Gerard McCloskey P.P., 2013 to date

Serving as a curate to Ballee between 1985 and 1988, the Rev. Fr. Gerry McCloskey spent a long part of his mission in the urban neighbourhoods of Belfast, firstly as curate at Ballymurphy until 1995, and then for six years in the Diocesan Cathedral, Saint Peter's. He succeeded to his first appointment as Parish Priest at Saint Agnes', in west Belfast, on 11 September 2001, a date etched on the minds of all of western civilisation when the twin towers in New York were destroyed. While Parish Priest there, he was called to the deathbed of a parishioner who told him the most exceptional story about the statue of Our Lady of Dunsford. And so, when he was appointed Parish Priest here on 22 August 2013, he realised that he was coming to the home of that statue. Fr. McCloskey had also served as Parish Priest at Holy Family for four years. He continues, as Fr. Fleck had done before him, without a curate.

ELEVEN
Sheepland

Sheepland is, in itself, an intriguing place name for, although the area may be rural in its nature, it has nothing whatsoever to do with sheep. The name actually derives from the Gaeilge Séipéalín[62] which means the little chapel and refers to the community of white friars who occupied the monastic site of Mullaghban, Mullach Bán, otherwise the white hill, this association being taken from the colour of the robes worn by the ecclesiastical people who lived there. For generations, it was also well known in the parish that there had been a very ancient monastic site at Crunglass[63]. Dr. Thomas Maitland Tate, who once lived in Seahornan and later rebuilt the Glebe House at Kilclief after a fire there in 1922, recorded many stories of the Sheepland area in his *Tales and Legends of Lecale,* one of which tells of the friars abandoning the monastery after it had been ravaged by the Danes. According to the traditional story they had melted down all of their gold.

It is easy to think of Norsemen as foreign invaders who carried out attacks at random in coastal areas, but these beliefs are modern misconceptions. They had actually begun to colonise different parts of Ireland and there is evidence, uncovered as recently as two years ago, of one of their settlements at nearby Kilclief, near the mouth of the sea inlet which they named Strang Fjord. Local place names still bear their origins in Norse such as, for example, Guns Island which derives from Gunnar Island, signifying a battle site. The word Viking, by which we usually refer to them, is also another modern name given to these people who, to the local populace, were known as the Fionn Gall and the Dubh Gall, otherwise the Fair Stranger and the Dark Stranger.

---

[62] The existence of the two townlands, Sheepland Beg and Sheepland More, is likely to have been the result of a land division for ecclesiastical purposes, and not because of two different chapels. This judgment is made from the survival of the Gaeilge tongue in the area and the fact that the two townlands were owned by different landlords.

[63] This place is mapped as Curraghglass and known locally by both this name, and Crunglass, which may be a name derived from the Gaeilge, Cruachan Glas, signifying a royal stronghold in a verdant landscape. There is also a third name, McAleastown, given to the cluster of houses, from the number of that family who lived there.

Many hundreds of years later, when Geordie Crean of Crunglass was repairing a field boundary built of stones and sods in the glen of Moneycam, he lifted a large stone and beneath it, and between two other stones, he came across a brown lump. He thought it felt weighty like a metal. "He brought it home in the evening and washed it, and on scraping part of it with a knife observed a bright yellow colour glittering through. He showed it to his wife. They decided to ask some of their neighbours to come in and see it. That night around the fire various opinions were expressed about its nature. Then an old man sitting in the corner recalled the legend of the Danes burning and destroying the monastery of Mullaghban nearby, and of the White Friars melting down their vessels and burying them before they fled. The effect of the story was instantaneous. Imagination was fired. Here was the hidden treasure."[64] The next day they set out for Downpatrick with the treasure:

> Looking across the long vista of years, we can see them on a bright spring morning sitting side by side in the low backed car; above them the lark with its joyous songs of promise, and hope finding an echo in their hearts.

Taking their find to a jeweller, they left it with him for valuation. However, when they returned the jeweller gave them news they didn't expect. "'It's made of a composition chiefly brass', he said. Their hearts sank. He offered them a bale of tobacco and a keg of rum in exchange, which they thought best to accept. They yoked the old grey mare in silence, and turned her head for home. Romance was dead."

The following morning however, the neighbours noticed that the jeweller hadn't opened his shop. As he lived alone concern began to grow and so his friends decided to enter the premises.

---

[64] Page 39, *Tales and Legends of Lecale*.

Nothing had been touched but the jeweller and the lump of gold were gone. He hadn't even felt the need to take anything else of value with him.

Although the monastery was deserted over a millennium ago, the name of Mullaghban has remained in the area ever since. The Mullaghban is a low and gentle knowe[65] which rises above the plain of farmland visible from the Sheepland Road. Even the well of the monastery was still discernible in the last century. Before the arrival of Christianity, the site at Crunglass was a celebrated Neolithic site with a nearby dolmen known as the Grey Stone, and just a little further south was Carraig-na-Capall, the rock of the Horse, which possibly took its name from a tribe of Pictish people who distinguished themselves by celebrating the horse as their figurehead.

The legend of this site demonstrates the rich culture of veneration which survived in the Sheepland area for centuries. When the Ordnance Survey Memoirs were commenced in the area, John O'Donovan was rather disheartened to discover, after speaking to Mr Martin, the antiquarian, then resident in Downpatrick, that the area of Lecale was inhabited largely by settlers. "He tells me that I can scarcely find one in the barony of Isle Lecale who speaks Irish, all the inhabitants being descendants of Scotch settlers, who know nothing of the names or antiquities of the place. I am told however there are still some insulated spots of aborigines around Ardglass." (24 April 1834).

On further discussion with Lieutenant Rimmington about the barony, O'Donovan wrote on 29 April 1834: "It is surprising to consider what intelligent people are to be met within these sequestered places and it is a fact that the more Irish they are, the more civil, obliging and intelligent you will find them and the more Scotch, the more reserved, cautious, cold, and un-obliging." The day when John O'Donovan was in the area of Ardglass with the two Benns, both from Saul, was unfortunately a rainy one which

---

[65] Pronounced 'noo'.

hindered their exploits. It can almost certainly be said, however, that the aborigines O'Donovan was so keen to encounter would have lived within Sheepland and Ardtole.

Despite this missed opportunity, fireside stories continued to be passed down from one generation to the next and enough of them survived to be published by Dr. Tate, although the thought of what has been lost remains a tantalising one. For most of his life James McAlea, of Crunglass, told his neighbours that there was a souterrain in Ciaran McConvey's field adjacent to the site of Mullaghban. He had often walked the field vainly trying to determine its location. Even before this there had been stone lined graves and stone cairns uncovered in the field, as the Rev. Monsignor James O'Laverty had noted in *An Historical Account of the Diocese of Down and Connor*. It wasn't until a month after James McAlea had died that a chance swipe of a mechanical digger laying a water main broke through the roof of the souterrain in March 1971.

The discovery was widely reported and even made page two of the next edition of the *Down Recorder* under the headline, *You never know what is underground*. A report was written up by Steven G. Rees-Jones, of Queen's University's archaeology department, assisted by his colleague, Patrick Collins of the Ministry of Finance, in the *Ulster Journal of Archaeology, 1971*. The passage was 100 feet long and laid out in a Y shaped plan with steps to clamber over and lintels to crawl under. At the centre of the complex was a round room, the roof of which the digger had broken through. This room would have been used as a store but could also have provided short-term shelter during raids on the site. The roof was soon repaired and the site covered over once again. In the years that followed, the local school children would skip class and spend the day in the cave.

At the time one of the locals, Jimmy Small, was interviewed, 'Most of us have known that there was an underground passage in that field but we never knew exactly where it was. James

McAlea walked the field many a time for he was sure it was there and unfortunately he died a short time ago. He would have been pleased to have been proved right'. Souterrains are not uncommon in Ireland and indeed in the same week there were three others found in various locations on the island.

Jimmy Small at the entrance to the soutterain. Image is reproduced by kind permission of the Down Recorder.

TWELVE
St Patrick's Well

Once a site of parish pilgrimages, this ancient well, created by our national apostle, sits on the rugged coast near Ardtole Church and is one of hundreds all over Ireland bearing the name of Saint Patrick. At low tide can be seen the natural rock outcrop, known as Saint Patrick's Road. This overhangs the sea giving the impression of a lost bridge across to the Isle of Man. The hagiographical tradition states that Saint Patrick created this formation. It was from here he would have completed his journey onwards to the island thirty miles across the sea, had it not been for a red-haired woman crossing his path without blessing it. This he considered to be a bad omen. A spot of white lichen on the rock here is said to be the remnants of his casula which he placed there. The proximity of Ardtole Church to the well could suggest that this edifice owes its foundation of the landing of Saint Patrick on the shore here.

The Rev. Monsignor O'Laverty records that "the banks of the little stream which flows from it are covered with bits of cloth which, according to ancient Celtic custom, have been cast into its waters or laid on its banks by the pilgrims." The origin of this custom stems from the simple notion that you have come to this site in need of healing, literally in bandages, which you then leave behind as a symbol of having completed your penance, and are therefore healed. Over time the tradition became thus that the pilgrims brought their bandages with them as a literal representation of their spiritual healing.

Long before *An Historical Account of the Diocese of Down and Connor* was written, a local historian by the name of Chambers records in his writings:

"In Sheepland is Saint Patrick's Well. Of its waters the good housewives are all so fond as to get some of its water before sunrise on May mornings to ensure a plentiful supply of milk and butter for the year."

This tradition would hark back to the pre-Christian era and the festival of Bealtaine. It will be remembered that in Sheepland the local people were privileged to enjoy an unbroken tradition,

PILGRIMAGE TO
ST. PATRICK'S WELL

Early twentieth century photograph of a pilgrimage.

not only of fluency in Irish but also the preservation of beliefs of an Ireland of long ago. Bealtaine in Gaeilge gives the month of May its name and it is on May Day that people would come from miles around to drown their mayflowers, otherwise known as the marsh marigold which nowadays are becoming increasingly rare. The drowned flowers would then be placed on the roofs of all the outbuildings on the farm to ward off evil spirits. In this month milk and butter would be plentiful and part of the ritual was to ensure that this continued throughout the summer. Poorer families would have had to rely on a solitary cow for sustenance and would have churned their own butter. And, for extra good fortune according to tradition, they would probably have had horseshoes nailed to the base of the churn. Surplus butter, if any, would have been sold at the butter market in Downpatrick, built in the middle of the 1800s.

The Rev. Canon J. J. Donnelly, who was appointed Parish Priest in January 1899, and who maintained the role until his death in 1927, made the well an assembly point on the Sunday when a mission closed. During these years there was a great revival of Irish customs in the parish mainly due to the enthusiastic efforts of Francis Joseph Bigger who, whilst remaining a Presbyterian, always supported local events within the Catholic parish. Missions were held every five years or so, and on the Sunday the band of the Ancient Order of Hibernians from Dunsford[66] would lead the procession towards the well. William Clark records a few different missions in his diary of events in the area, one reads:

"Father Joseph of the Passionist Order on May 15th 1904 began a mission of two weeks duration in Dunsford Parish, the first week in Ardglass ending on May 22nd next week in Dunsford ending May 29th being a great success nearly all in the parish joining the anti-treating league ending with the renewal of baptismal vows and lighted candles. 700 being present. It was a great success spiritually for the people."

Father Joseph of the Passionist Order on May 15th 1904 began a mission of two weeks duration in Dunsford Parish, the first week in Ardglass ending on May 22nd next week in Dunsford ending May 29th being a great success nearly all in the parish joining the anti-treating league ending with the renewal of baptismal vows and lighted candles. 700 being present."

During the 1958 renovations carried out by the Saint Vincent de Paul chapter in the parish, a crucifix was presented by the Rev. Fr. Pat McAlea. This came from Saint Mary's in Belfast, where he

---

[66] The Ancient Order of Hibernians had a hall beside the Church of Ireland where people from all over the parish would gather to watch shows and listen to band recitals. An account of the events hosted at the A.O.H. Hall can be found in *Before it's too late* by Willie Crea.

AT ST. PATRICK'S WELL, DUNSFORD, CO. DOWN.
Four-group on Platform—from the left—No. 1, Mr. BIGGER; No. 3, FATHER DONNELLY, P.P.

A pilgrimage to the well when Francis Joseph Bigger was resident in Jordan's Castle. Included is the band of the Ancient Order of Hibernians of Dunsford. Both this image and the one on page 165 were taken by John MacMahon.

was then administrator. The bottom of the well was secured by a millstone which was presented by Bella Curran and a second well was created with a sandstone bowl. This was the gift of Dennis Breen of Killard. The well has remained much the same to this day.

This place, however, is not the only site in the parish which can claim an association with the national saint. Tradition has it that the first sermon preached in the parish was by Saint Patrick himself at the rocks off Killard Point where he prayed to the fish on his way into Strangford Lough before landing at the Slaney river in 432 AD. The tradition also claims that these rocks and Rock Angus were once one and were separated by Saint Patrick's boat passing through.

A third hagiographical tradition relating to this parish states that Saint Patrick made it his mission to visit all the local chieftains and in so doing he encountered the MacDhu of Ardglass. The chief of the clan was unimpressed and decided to walk Saint Patrick back to Saul. But he soon came round to the words of Saint Patrick and told him that he would allow himself, and all of his followers, to be baptised by him there and then, provided a source of water could be found. Saint Patrick, seeing that there was none, painlessly pierced the man's foot with his staff. The blood which flowed forth he then commanded to turn to water and the chieftain and all of his followers were then baptised. This stream has never ceased to flow since that day and, from its name, the Stream of Blood, tSruth bhFuile, it has become known as none other than the famous Struell Wells[67].

---

[67] This tradition is taken from *Belfast Magazine and Literary Journal* published on 1 March 1825. Another variation on this version states that Saint Brigid was walking with Saint Patrick through the area one day. Wishing to quench her thirst she asked Patrick to procure a source of water. The foot of one of the members of the group was pierced just as in the above tradition.

THIRTEEN
Ardtole Church

Ardtole takes its name from the given name, Tuathail. According to the interpretation of the Northern Ireland Environment Agency, he was in fact the legendary Gaeilge monarch Tuathail Techtmar who lived in the second century and who founded the ancient province of Meath. The Ward[68] of Ardtole is a prominence overlooking from the east the Irish Sea, Ardglass and Saint John's Point to the south with the Mournes as the backdrop. The panorama extends across the glacial basin of the Lecale peninsula towards Slieve-na-Griddle and Castlemahon. The selection of the site of Ardtole church was similar to that of the ancient Druid monuments[69]. By this time too, Christianity was beginning to assert itself on the landscape and amongst the people of the area.

A view of Ardtole church from the east.

---

[68] Ward is from the old English 'weard', guarding post or outlook. In modern etymology warden has the same stem.

[69] On the crest of the Strangford Road just before the descent into Ardglass, there is an ancient site known as the Cross of Ardtole which would lead one to the assumption that this was a Christian site. However, on the contrary, it is the site of a Neolithic tomb and, on reflection, an ideal site for such a monument with its excellent views, similar to those of the church. The monument survives as a D shaped mound, approximately one and a half metres in width and three in length, and stands one and a half metres in height from the south west and almost three metres from the north east. Described as 'sitting atop a dry stone passage', the mound is capped by two large stone slabs. Sadly, in recent years, the site has suffered damage from the encroaching plough.

The ancient cross slab of Ardtole, which is located above the front door of Saint Mary's and dates from the tenth century, comes from an era when, because of the constant plundering and marauding by Norsemen, it would have been both vital and necessary to use the adjacent souterrain to the south west of the church. The existence of this ancient tunnel affirms the fact that Ardtole is one of the earliest Christian sites in the area. The souterrain was only rediscovered when a hole appeared in the adjacent field. The cause of this was a lintel, which made up part of the roof, collapsing. This revealed, for the first time in centuries, a thirty metre long curving tunnel. After the discovery it was photographed by Robert John Welsh who, using his intuition, placed paper on the floor to reflect the sunlight as a means of lighting up the tunnel, thus creating a very atmospheric photograph.

The preservation of the church structure was the result of another of Francis Joseph Bigger's Lecale projects. He started the work in 1914 and the church, as we see it today, had more than likely been constructed in the fourteenth century, going by the age of the glass. The building itself measures twenty-one feet by sixty-three. The western side of the church has been levelled to below sill height and the earth lying on the gable became a means of protecting the building from its exposed position. From the exterior the north door, which was protected by its drawbar set into the wall, steps down into the western end of the building. During his excavations, Frank came to the conclusion that this part may have been a residence with an entrance through either the north or the second south door. Once inside the structure, the full extent of the impressive eastern gable, with its large gothic arch which can be seen for miles, can be appreciated. The glass which had illuminated the windows was discovered on the floor during Bigger's excavations. At the time of its uncovering it was not only the oldest glass found on the island but also the largest collection. Today these fragments are held in the vaults of the National Museum of Ireland in Kildare Street, Dublin.

In his journal about the work, Francis Joseph Bigger writes:

> None of the mullions remain, so it is very hard to say what form they took. The glass itself has excited a keen interest, as it is believed to be the oldest found in Ireland, and may have been made in this country, but at present there is no positive proof of this.

The east window of Ardtole church.

Medieval glass expert of the era, Dudley Westropp, reported:

> A good many portions bear portions of design in 'enamel brown' and one may ... be ornamented in 'silver

stain' which was introduced early in the 14th century. All the pieces are roughly chipped to the required shape, which indicates their age. Cutting glass by the diamond was not done till the 17th century. Most of the glass is of greenish colour, some very dark, a few pieces are of a fine sapphire blue and two pieces of ruby glass show the method of making – viz. clear glass in the centre with a layer of ruby glass on either side.

The decoration on the glass includes the regal Fleur de Lis pattern, accompanied by wonderful foliage, somewhat reminiscent of the fern which adorns the picturesque ruin. The final decoration, which I could discern were floral motifs, reminded me of the lotus flower which remarkably had a similar appearance to the Art Nouveau style, and all this goes to show how decorative fashions can transcend centuries. Amongst these small fragmentary remains, decorated glass borders can also be seen.

However beautiful the glass though, the lack of mullions means that it is impossible to ascertain how the windows were fashioned. Today the east window frames the maritime horizon punctuated by the Isle of Man. Vessels from Ardglass harbour often pass under the watch of the church which is dedicated to Saint Nicholas[70], the patron saint of sailors.

The congregation served by the church was a largely rural community engaged in agriculture. Following a dispute with the chief of the McCartan clan over the price of animals, the burgesses of Ardglass found him drunk and tied him to the briars by the wisps of his long beard. When he awoke, he had to cut himself free

---

[70] Such a dedication could not however predate the twelfth century when the relics of the saint were re-enshrined at Bari. Since this, the relics of Saint Nicholas were brought to the lost town of Newtown Jerpoint by descendants of the crusading de Frainet family. They were buried there in 1200 and remain there to this day. It is remarkable that throughout our western world there are three saints celebrated in many cultures, Saint Nicholas, Saint Valentine, and Saint Patrick and that Ireland can hold claim on all three, as Saint Valentine is buried in Dublin.

thereby losing his beard, the symbol of his social standing. Much like Samson when his hair was cut, he had to regain his authority. Thoroughly infuriated, he incited his clan to avenge the insult and they set out for Ardtole where they massacred the congregation assembled for Midnight Mass. The site has remained abandoned ever since.

Jonathan Swift's *Gulliver's Travels*, written in 1726, drew inspiration from the story of the McCartan chief's vengeance and wrote, "At the place where the carriage stopt, there stood an

The north door of Ardtole church.

ancient temple, esteemed to be the largest in the whole kingdom, which having been polluted some years before by an unnatural murder ... In this edifice it was determined I should lodge."

The map of English Ardtole of 1768 shows the church sitting in its own enclosure in an open field. The site, once renowned for its collection of black and white maidenhair ferns, was, at that time, still revered as a sacred site by those who lived in the area, and the condition of the church has remained much the same for the last few centuries. This was affirmed by the fact that Francis Joseph Bigger was condemned for being overzealous in his contemporary efforts at Saint Tassach's church in Raholp. There his efforts were considered to have been a little too enthusiastic, because he had actually rebuilt some parts of the church.

ARDTOLE CHURCH.

As I stood by old Ardtole Church on a lovely summer's day
And watched the fishing fleet put in again to Ardglass bay
The gulls were wheeling all around how piercing was their cry
I closed my eyes and there did dream of other days gone by.

Now the scene did change as I stood upon that mound
To pay their homage to the Lord the faithful gathered round
While some menfolk a watch did keep for those who'd shoot to kill
And many a warning shout was heard upon the holy hill.

There were McBartans and Maginness's good honest men and true
Still what happened on that fateful morn no one ever knew
Those gathered there were butchered upon that grassy knoll
And left their ghosts to hover round the ruins of old Ardtole.

These lines were written by Clement Digney.

179

During his excavations Frank had cleared the floor of the debris but could not find any trace of burning or of any bodies. This led him to mistakenly conclude that the massacre may not have actually happened; a fact which he backed up with the claim that there was no record of the incident during the 1640s, the time when he believed that it may have occurred. But, unknown to him, the massacre had actually taken place at the end of the 1400s.

What Frank did find were the glass fragments and a few other artefacts. A key, the carved hand of a bishop giving a blessing, and a glass bead which was most likely jewellery from one of the parishioners. The carved hand was preserved and inserted above the gospel side of the altar. It was unique in that it had the appearance of being complete in itself, meaning that it had never been part of a statue. Unfortunately, it was taken at some stage and has never been recovered although a replica carving was made in 2013 and is on display at Down County Museum.

FOURTEEN
Our Lady of Dunsford

'Naom Muire an Dunseford' reads the inscribed pedestal on which stands the only existing pre-Reformation stone statue of the Madonna and Child on the island of Ireland. The remarkable legend of this unique relic of medieval Irish Christianity begins at a quarry in Scrabo, at the head of Strangford Lough from where the sandstone was extracted. Examination of the carving on the limbs and robes of the statue concludes that it is not dissimilar to one of Affreca, princess of the Isle of Man and wife of John de Courcy, to be found at Greyabbey. The implication of this is that monks based there carved the statue and it was given to the medieval church at Dunsford. Life-size statues such as this were very common in continental Europe in the early fourteenth century, and Our Lady of Dunsford is a contemporary of these dating from around the year 1300.

The Virgin Mary has always been a central figure in Christianity but she became particularly important during the medieval era. She was revered and venerated as an intercessor for the salvation of humankind. As the mother of Christ, she was also a model for all mothers in general. When shown with Christ and her mother Anne, she provided an ideal example of religious family life. In Passion images, Mary invites onlookers to share her grief and suffering at the death of her son.

From the church site[71] at Dunsford people walked in a procession to stone crosses to the west of the church along an old pathway. A smaller cross was located in a field originally belonging to the Hanna family.[72] Another, an Crois Mór, was on the farm

---

[71] Henry Fitzsimons, the author's grandfather, believed that there may have been a souterrain under Church Road, at the front of the church. His reason for believing this was that anytime he passed the front of the building towing his old horse-drawn reaper, the blade would vibrate in an unusual way, as if the ground beneath was hollow. It has never been stated that Rogerus de Dunesford founded the church, merely that he had granted the church that stood there to the Abbey of Saint Patrick in 1194. It could be possible that this church site too was an early Christian one.

[72] The sites of the crosses are no longer discernible. There were two groves (the one on the Hanna farm has long since been removed) which were planted on both farms, and it is believed that the crosses may have been located there.

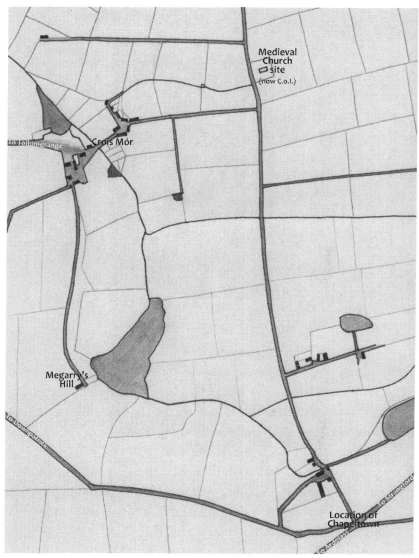

Dunsford and Ballyedock c.1760. Drawn by the author.

originally belonging to the Smyth family who were the ancestors of the present Fitzsimons occupiers. On the Smyth farm there was also a holy spring known as Mary's Well, about which the author's grandfather informed Betty McCord. It was largely due

Crossmore c.1960. Photograph courtesy of Kevin Crangle.

to the efforts of Betty that the field names of this parish were recorded for posterity. The site of the well is thought to be under the foreground outhouses[73] as shown on the aerial photograph of the site, which dates from about 1960.

This church at Dunsford is believed to have been among the most highly decorated in the district of Lecale[74]. However, after the proclamation of the Act of Supremacy by Henry VIII, the situation the church found itself in became rather confused. The statue was broken up and left in pieces at the site. A few different citations point the finger of blame at a soldier of Oliver Cromwell's army. The feet and torso were removed from the church at Dunsford and carried to the residence of the Rev. Dr. William Megarry[75], Parish

[73] This has been determined by a spring which rises through the floor of these buildings.
[74] This fact has been determined by the discovery of mullion fragments from the windows, as well as the existence of the statue.
[75] Overlooking Crossmore and the church site is Megarry's Hill, where the Rev. Dr. William may well have resided with his family when he was ministering to the Parish

Priest of Dunsford and Ardglass. He had been born at Crossmore and removed these pieces in order to conceal the fragments from destructive hands.

Following Dr. Megarry's death in 1763, his remains were interred at Dunsford churchyard. After losing their guardian, the portions of the statue were carried to the Newark in Ardglass. On the map of the town in the *Survey of the Manor of Ardglass*, it is recorded that, in 1768, the range of medieval buildings now incorporated into Ardglass Castle was known as the monastery. Whether it was due to the remnants of Our Lady of Dunsford there present, or the confusion of the cell-like structure of the rooms with their gothic arches, we cannot be certain.

The head of the statue of Our Lady was found in the medieval churchyard before the erection of the new chapel was begun in 1791. This lone fragment was inserted into the gable by the Rev. Fr. Edward Mulholland. The head was clearly still held in great veneration by the people of the parish. In 1886, Robert Burns of Killough wrote the verses on this card (shown right) as part of his eulogy for his aunt, Mrs. Margaret Martin of Lismore, who was buried beneath the steeple of the chapel[76].

---

of Dunsford and Ardglass. The dwelling is shown on the 1768 *Survey of the Manor of Ardglass*.

[76] Mrs. Margaret Martin was the sister of John Fitzsimons and she was the first person known to have been buried in that plot and her name can be found on the side of the headstone.

The building range, of which the Newark comprised, was subsequently redeveloped in 1789 by Rear Admiral Lord Charles James FitzGerald, into Ardglass Castle. Charles Lilley was appointed as his architect. Lilley was a man with a penchant for repurposing medieval building structures, as it was he who drew up the plans for the Cathedral of the Holy Trinity in Downpatrick. It is quite probable that Lord Charles approached him at the time of his appointment.

Major Aubrey William Beauclerk was Lord Charles' half-nephew and Victorian successor to the landlordship of Ardglass. As a man of impressive social standing, Major Beauclerk would hold several engagements at his County Down seat. Ardglass, with its other five castles, must have proved quite a marvel to a Victorian visitor. Fashionable tastes for the upper classes at that time transcended the Romantic Movement which favoured tumbledown ruins. Follies were the 'in thing' and included reinterpreting ruined antiquity. The creations of the movement were images reminiscent of the ancient Roman Forum and the Acropolis. Unique to Major Beauclerk's pleasure grounds was a ruined statue and, from studying its restored state, it can be seen that the lower fragment of Our Lady of Dunsford would have stood to thigh height as his Victorian folly.

Unfortunately for Major Beauclerk and the populace of the Ardglass estate, his son and heir did not have the same sensibilities or love for the family seat. The castle was put up for rent and lay derelict and neglected for long periods while Aubrey de Vere Beauclerk was off gallivanting, frivolously frittering away the estate his father and great grandfather had tended so dearly. Ardglass Castle was abandoned and the gardens left untended. In 1896 a lease was agreed and the first seven holes of Ardglass golf course were laid out. Amusingly, at the same time the Belfast and County Down Railway was leased the ground also. There is even an account of a disgruntled day tripper having her cup of tea smashed out of her hand and left holding only the porcelain handle. One night vandals entered the pleasure grounds and destroyed the folly. They carried off the statue and hurled it into the sea beneath the first tee of the course.

In June 2009 the Rev. Fr. Gerard McCloskey, working as Parish Priest of Saint Agnes' parish at the time, received a telephone call from a parishioner regarding his father, Terry Hamill, who was ill. Fr. McCloskey was asked to bring a Dictaphone as Terry knew of a family story regarding the statue, which went something like this:

> In 1905, the golf club's greenkeeper, Joseph Hamill, Terry's grandfather, was tasked with re-landscaping part of one of the greens. This involved relocating some steps within what had been part of Ardglass Castle's front lawn. Late into the afternoon he overturned one of the steps and discovered that its underside was intricately carved. He immediately realised the significance of his discovery, so he replaced it and told no one about it.
>
> That night he woke his ten-year-old son John and, under cover of darkness, they went out to the steps with a wheelbarrow and a shovel. After hoisting it on to the wheelbarrow and bringing it back to their house in Castle Place, they decided that it would best be placed under John's bed. The presence of the fragment terrified John as he waited with baited breath for someone to come looking for it.
>
> Four to six weeks later, when they were sure the stone had not been missed, they decided what should be done. Joseph and John brought out the wheelbarrow and placed sacking around the wheel in order to deaden any noise. Having lifted the stone on to it, again in the dark, they wheeled it to Chapeltown, two miles distant, and left it at the church.

Whether he knew it or not, Charles Lilley has seemingly had a hand in obscuring two great parts of Lecale's heritage. The first was that when he undertook the work at Down Cathedral, he cleared the interior of all graves. This included that of Saints Patrick, Brigid, and Columba. Of course, the second was when he accidentally incorporated Our Lady of Dunsford into a garden feature.

Francis Joseph Bigger was at that time a frequent visitor to Lecale. He would have sleuthed around and worked out, from written text and gathering oral tradition, what had become of the notable statue. With his expert eye, he was able to identify the fragments as parts of the statue. This meant that he had succeeded where many, including the Rev. Dr. Richard Marner, who was Parish Priest from 1876 to 1885, had failed. Frank could then claim success, as the torso had now been located having been missing for almost a century and a half. He recounted, 'Fortune favoured me in gathering them together, my antiquarian experience readily recognising carved fragments of an ancient statue in what to others might only have appeared as "old stones"'. Having gathered all the pieces together, the statue was reassembled by Robert May of Belfast with modern heads[77] and inserted into the gable by S. & T. Hastings at Chapeltown on 25 March 1908. This was the Feast of the Annunciation and a special feature of the ceremony was the free use of the Gaeilge tongue.

The joy in the parish was palpable for weeks beforehand. The children of Saint Mary's Dunsford National School were given lyrics to learn which their teacher Mary Mount had penned. Miss Mount, who later married a man by the name of Halpin, was a

---

[77] The head of Jesus has never been located although the author's grandfather thought that it might be found in the field immediately in front of the medieval church site. Nor has the hand of Our Lady ever been located either. It has also never been stated where the original head of Our Lady had been found – the one inserted by the Rev. Fr. Mulholland – nor where it went to. However, if you pay attention to the gateway at the quayside entrance to Jordan's Castle, you will discover a carved head of a female, see the photograph on page 48. This archway was erected in 1911 and the head inserted there, and this, perhaps, was when it was finally returned to its parish.

A group of girls who formed the choir at the unveiling of the restored shrine of Our Lady of Dunsford. The photograph was taken by John MacMahon and included among the group is a young Mrs Halpin.

talented musician who composed numerous songs. She is fondly remembered for sitting around the harmonium with the children. So skilled was she that any verse could be matched to a tune. The choir of Saint Mary's would sing a variation of her hymn at both Easter and Christmas to the tune of *O Little Town of Bethlehem*[78]:

> Facing the east our statue stands
> On a hilltop by the sea.
> Profaned and torn by strife in the past
> But restored now that all might see

[78] As currently played by Una Fitzsimons, this version has been varied a little and the tune which accompanies the lyrics has been adapted from a waltz which Gerry Curran's band composed and it has ever since been elevated to the role of this parish's indigenous hymn.

The image of Mary, favoured by grace,
Mother of God's own Son,
Our Lady of Dunsford, plead for us
Till salvation's battle be won.

As we pass by your shrine both day and night
On our earthly business bent,
May we offer a prayer to your listening ear
For your special kind of grace,
That peace may reign in our own dear land
Where Ireland's saint adored.
O Lady of Dunsford, plead for us,
God hearkens to your every word.

The work was once again made famous throughout Ireland, from northeast to south west, by Francis Joseph Bigger. This is a reference to it in the *Journal of the Cork Historical and Archaeological Society* in 1913:

"This statue had been shattered and scattered, and all traces of it had disappeared for centuries. It is like a romance. Mr. Bigger searched for them and found them broken into three main portions in various places. One was in the doorstep of a golf club house. The tale is too long to tell, but suffice to say, he rescued the "disjecta membra," and had them rejoined by a capable workman in Belfast, and replaced in a niche over the west doorway of St. Mary's Dunsfort."

For the Marian Year 1954, Canon McKee, who had two Marian shrines, made Our Lady of Dunsford something special to celebrate. While many parishes erected Lourdes grottos, Dunsford and Ardglass printed calendars featuring Our Lady of Dunsford. Some of these calendars, which were sold for 1s.6d., are still to be found adorning walls of homes in the area. As one of the most ancient stone Madonnas in the world, the statue is unique in Ireland in that it is still venerated by its original parish. In August 2013, by a strange twist of fate, Fr. Gerard McCloskey , as Parish Priest, found himself in the role of Guardian of the Restored Shrine of Our Lady of Dunsford and Protector of the Holy Well of Saint Patrick. It is thanks to him that we can now record for posterity the story of the parish's most ancient resident.

In Memory of Mrs Martin Lismore

Almost within sight of the wild Irish coast
Whose billows the rocky coast lave
And just on the verge of the broad country road
Youll notice a newly made grave

A few scattered houses surround the churchyard
From which a neat Church rears its head
As a Mother broods over the loss of her young
It ever keeps watch oer the dead

Although there is naught in the view Picturesque
And most unromantic the scene
Yet the memory of Her who sleeps there will remain
In the hearts of Her friends ever green

For there in that habitation of clay
And deep in the Earths chilly breast
Repose the remains of Her who was once
Of Mothers the kindest and best

But in dear old Lismore there's a vacancy now
That will never again be filled up
With sorrow our hearts are nigh broken to day
And brimful of grief is our cup

Now we loved Her is known at last
Although Her best virtues we thought we all knew
Oh yes the mill wheel never never can turn
With the water that flowing has passed

Robert Burns Killough

Bibliography

Aalen, F.H.A.; Whelan, K.; Stout, M.; 1997, *Atlas of the Irish rural landscape*, Cork University Press, Cork.

Burdy, Rev. S.; 1802, *Ardglass or the Ruined Castles*, Graisberry and Campbell, Dublin.

Clark, R.; 1832-1858, *Diary of life in Ardglass and its neighbourhood*.

Clark, W.; 1870-1907, *Diary of Births, Deaths, and Marriages in Ardglass and its neighbourhood*.

Crea, W.; 2003, *Before it's too late*, Down Recorder, Downpatrick.

Crolly, Rev. G.; 1851, *The Life of the Most Rev. Doctor Crolly*, James Duffy, Dublin.

Flanders, S.; 2014, *John de Courcy: Prince of Ulster*, Colourpoint, Newtownards.

Gill Sharp, M.; 2012, *Moonlight on Ballyhornan Bay*, April Sky Design, Newtownards.

Holohan, P.; 1973, *Ireland Two*, The Educational Company of Ireland Limited, Dublin.

Irish News Archive.

Macauley, Rev. A.; 2000, *Down and Connor: A Short History*, Belfast.

Rankin, J.F.; 1997, *Down Cathedral*, Ulster Historical Foundation, Belfast.

O'Kelly, P.; 1844, *The History of Ireland*, James Duffy, Dublin.

O'Laverty, Rev. J.; 1878, *An Historical Account of the Diocese of Down and Connor, Vol. I*, James Duffy, Dublin.

O'Laverty, Rev. J.; 1880, *An Historical Account of the Diocese of Down and Connor, Vol. II*, James Duffy, Dublin.

Partridge, J.; 2010, *Representations and Transformations of Synagoga*, University of East Anglia.

Rice, G.; 1991, *St. Mary's Roman Catholic Church Dunsford 1791-1991*, Shanway Press, Belfast.

Smyth, D.; 2009, *Market Street*, Lagan Press, Belfast.

Tate, Dr. T.M.; [No date], *Tales and Legends of Lecale Co. Down*, Down Recorder, Downpatrick.

Various authors; 1962, *St. Patrick's Church, Ballyphillip, Portaferry*, P. Quinn & Co. Ltd.

Various authors; 2013, *A Harvest of History from Dunsford and Ardglass, Vol. I*, Flixx Graphics, Downpatrick.